.the
Voice
of a
Child

In the Voice of a Child

JUDY EMERSON

THOMAS NELSON PUBLISHERS

Nashville

Published in Nashville, Tennessee, by Thomas Nelson, Inc.

Scripture quotations noted NKJV are from THE NEW KING JAMES VERSION. Copyright © 1979, 1980, 1982, Thomas Nelson, Inc., Publishers.

Scripture quotations noted KJV are from The Holy Bible, KING JAMES VERSION.

Scripture quotations noted NIV are taken from the HOLY BIBLE, NEW INTERNATIONAL VERSION ®. Copyright © 1973, 1978, 1984 by International Bible Society. Used by permission of Zondervan Bible Publishing House. All rights reserved.

The "NIV" and "New International Version" trademarks are registered in the United States Patent and Trademark Office by International Bible Society. Use of either trademark requires the permission of International Bible Society.

Scripture quotations noted TLB are from *The Living Bible* (Wheaton, Illinois: Tyndale House Publishers, 1971) and are used by permission.

Library of Congress Cataloging-in-Publication Data

Emerson, Judy.

In the voice of a child / Judy Emerson.

p. cm.

ISBN 0–8407–4504–4 (pbk.)

1. Adult child sexual abuse victims—Pastoral counseling of—Case studies.   2. Adult child sexual abuse victims—Religious life.   3. Emerson, Judy.   4. Spiritual life—Christianity.   I. Title

BV4596.A25E54   1994

261.8'32—dc20   93-42520
                                                                              CIP

Printed in the United States of America
1 2 3 4 5 6 7—99 98 97 96 95 94

DEDICATION

This book is dedicated to you who are still burdened with the sufferings of the wounded child within you. I pray for your healing.

"I pray also that the eyes of your heart may be enlightened in order that you may know the hope to which He has called you" (Ephesians 1:18, NIV).

INTRODUCTION

The following pages are taken from a personal journal I kept during two years of psychotherapy with a Christian counselor, working to overcome the effects of childhood incest. My decision to share them publicly, in my own name, is based on my conviction that it is time for the secrecy that crushes the lives of incest victims to be brought to light. It is in the light that we confess our shame and find ourselves accepted even with all of the dirtiness we may feel. Only in the light can we be healed and finally reclaim our lost innocence.

Our cultural unwillingness to know about sexual abuse has conspired with abusers to perpetuate the intergenerational cycle of crimes against children. Silence has kept their offenses cloaked in darkness. "For everyone practicing evil hates the light and does not come to the light, lest his deeds should be exposed" (John 3:20, NKJV). Yet I am thankful that "God is light and in Him is no darkness at all" (1 John 1:5, NKJV). The darkness has been overcome. The evil has been confronted.

In these pages I offer you a glimpse of the shame that debilitated my life for nearly thirty years. It cannot hurt me any longer, but perhaps its telling can be a part of the healing of others who suffer. I am no longer ashamed to own my story.

My family may feel differently, however. To protect their anonymity, I have changed all names in the book except my own, and omitted identifying details. Each of them has the freedom to privately acknowledge or deny my experience. Their response will not change the truth. If they experience hurt after reading what I have written, I believe it will be a result of the resurfacing of their own ever-present shame, carried from the inception of their own childhood wounds, and from the wounds they inflicted in others. Perhaps the light cast on that shame will serve as a catalyst for their choices to find a path toward healing for themselves. That is my prayer.

No one has a moment-by-moment recollection of all the events of their early years. Survivors of sexual abuse often find memory gaps of an even greater degree due to repression of trauma. My memories of the events over those years are, of course, incomplete. The purpose of this book is not complete detailed documentation of events, nor confrontation, but healing in the heart of one who experiences pain.

For most of my life I said about my childhood, "Well, it wasn't what I wanted it to be, but it wasn't *that* bad." Indeed, there are many life stories more horrifying than my own. While I was spared the extreme physical brutality that many children endure, my story illustrates the violence done to a child's soul when she is stripped of her human right to be in control of her own body. No matter how subtle the coercion that precedes the sexual assault of a child, profound emotional damage results. Yet, as long as we minimize our hurt by sheathing it in insulating generalities, we deny the need for healing balm and the wound continues to fester untreated.

In acknowledging and examining our wounds we discover a hidden "inner child"—that part of us who received the hurts—and almost uncontrollably continues to act spontaneously on her true feelings, rather than to act with rational "adult" deliberation. I wonder if that was the apostle Paul's inner child in action when he said, "what I am doing, I do not understand. For what I will to do, that I do not practice; but what I hate, that I do" (Romans 7:15, NKJV). Perhaps another angle from which to view what Paul referred to as the sin dwelling in us might be as a natural, wounded child who reacts to stresses inappropriately, thus, as sin is defined, "misses the mark"? Gratefully, "God demonstrates His own love toward us, in that *while we were still sinners,* Christ died for us" (Romans 5:8, NKJV, emphasis mine). He didn't wait to love us until we had matured into being naturally "good" people.

Jesus had a special place in His heart for little children. He sought to protect them, and He was patient with their interruptions. He understood that their immaturity, while far from His purpose for them, was suitable to the development they had not yet been able to attain. Knowing that children are not yet complete, He modeled for us perfect parental love and acceptance for imperfect children. It was a model we might well use in learning to accept our own inner children too.

Of course, growth and maturity are goals we all need. It is good to change behavior patterns that hurt others and ourselves into more effective ways of relating. But Jesus changed the hearts of those He met by accepting them as they are, gently opening their eyes to a better way. Are we as gentle with ourselves as Jesus would be with us? Or do we try to force that inner child to shut up and let the adult in us do the talking?

Paul gave us a wonderful example in the love chapter, 1 Corinthians 13:11 (NKJV), "When I was a child, I spoke as a child, I understood as a child, I thought as a child; but when I became a man, I put away childish things." He speaks of "putting away" behaviors that were no longer appropriate. Yet, for anything we must put away, as we put away laundry, there is a process which requires us to acknowledge the existence of the laundry, to consider our means of dealing with it, to sort and handle it, to mentally and physically organize it and store it. The process of handling the laundry may allow us to change our perspective on it, as we might discover a torn rag and choose to discard it, even though our previous perception of that rag might have been of a favorite shirt which had seen better days.

Putting away laundry doesn't happen on its own, just because we will it to be done. And if we chose to simply act as if the laundry didn't exist, we'd be in a mess very soon, like we sometimes get into a mess by trying to deny our childishness as an ineffective way of getting beyond it.

Childishness is not an attractive, mature attribute in a grown person. In that respect, the inner child certainly has great need to grow and learn. But childlikeness is an admirable quality of purity, vulnerability, and willingness to trust. Perhaps that quality was in Jesus' message when He said that unless you "become as little children, you will by no means enter the kingdom of heaven" (Matthew 18:3, NKJV).

For myself, I had to learn to acknowledge my childishness in order to find my childlikeness. In the process of my counseling, I became aware for the first time of my dissociation, or splitting, from my adult self when under stress. Even while conscious of myself as an adult in her mid-thirties, I found myself thinking in the voice of a small frightened child, who, for the purposes of the printed page, I refer to as *judy*.

I became increasingly attuned to my inner child's presence as I gave her opportunities to share her feelings without judgment. "*Yuu-uuuck!*" she would often say inside my head as a reaction to a shameful topic she was afraid to think about. I learned to listen sympathetically to her terror, and her innocence, to respect the pain she experienced, and to admire her strength in coping with it. Eventually she felt accepted, safe, and loved enough to give up some of the rebellious control she had exerted over my behavior. She trusted me enough to let the adult me choose a healthier course of action. It was true repentance.

Of course, many people have received helpful counseling with only superficial or no inquiry at all into their childhood history. Perhaps some can benefit from little more than a swift kick in the pants to motivate them to look at their own responsibility in their difficulties. But such methods, however effective they appear to be in those cases, may simply serve to drive those who have been more deeply wounded further into their hopelessness. The healing process for two individuals who suffer, relatively speaking, from a head cold and a case of leukemia, will necessarily have different lengths, and require different kinds of attention for real change to occur. Only a counselor experienced with healing deep trauma may be able to recognize the symptoms of such inner pain. Referral to a knowledgeable professional may be the best choice for counselors who have never before encountered clients who have been sexually victimized.

Some readers may be concerned about the danger of overfocus on the past. Before I began therapy, even though I was unable to articulate my pain, my entire life had been unconsciously focused on a childish wish for retribution, a greedy striving for my unmet needs to be attended to, and a compressed, but all-encompassing rage. It was during those years that I was overfocused on the past. Therapy was my first opportunity to enter the grief process that should have been allowed when I was a little girl, each time I was wrongly used. There were many years of unexpressed loss that needed to be vented in the context of a supportive, appropriate relationship that could help me release the feelings and move beyond them into a greater maturity, unburdened of the excess baggage, and ready to forgive.

Ecclesiastes 3:1 (NKJV) tells us "To everything there is a season, a time for every purpose under heaven." Long delayed, God had finally led me to the season for me to mourn a litany of my losses as a child. The season did end eventually, after two years of intense therapy, and another year of grief work on my own. I continued to accept my inner child as she was, not hurrying her process of moving through the feelings she needed to feel. Eventually her pain was spent. She has found peace with the past.

My healing required three years of my adult life. But don't assume this to be an ideal of how therapy "should" take place. Many survivors of child sexual abuse spend much longer than I needed. Some need less time. Each person works at her own pace, and each person has a varying history of traumatic experience which she must mourn. In God's time our grief will subside, only after the buried feelings have all found their way to consciousness for release.

The emotions expressed in the pages of my journal were scribbled fresh as they welled up from inside me. Editing for publication as a book has been with the intention of organizing and clarifying the message of hope that emerged through the pain. But the rawness of those feelings has been intentionally preserved, because incest victims must find a safe way to verbalize whatever shame-infected ideas they discover, in order to clean the wounds. Editing the thoughts as they appear in our minds only keeps them secret, and powerful.

The rawness also serves to demonstrate the process by which I was eventually able to put a great deal of childish thought into its proper perspective. I have not amended the warped, "wrong" viewpoints I expressed. The reader is invited into my mental turbulence in order to understand its sources, and to rejoice with me as I was freed from it, and enabled to change.

The therapist I call "Jason," who helped me to find my way through that turbulence, is a gifted counselor whose faith was a model for my own growth. I will always be grateful for his skills. Yet at the same time, I found that working on my issues about sexuality with the member of the gender that abused me presented a set of challenges all its own.

Perhaps it was to my personal benefit that I was repeatedly required to acknowledge how confused was my understanding of male-female relationships. In spite of that, I would caution victims of sexual abuse to seek a therapist of their own gender. The experience of therapy is by its very nature one of extreme intimacy. Under such conditions, feelings of attraction in both client and therapist are perfectly natural and common.

Developing trust with one's counselor is the foundation for the ability to bring out all the toxic shame that has been hidden for so long. When that long-defended fortress surrounding our wounded sexuality finally begins to crumble, we are vulnerable to a degree we cannot recognize at the time. An opposite-sex therapist has an enormous responsibility to guard his own responses to the client, while protecting her vulnerability. Not all counselors can manage such a challenge, and some, consciously or unconsciously, betray the trust of their clients. The risk of re-abuse is real.

I am grateful that my experience of therapy with a male, while excruciatingly difficult at times, was one of safety and protection. Jason temporarily filled the roles of parent, teacher, friend, cheerleader, and advocate. He demonstrated God's love for me.

One aspect of our work together is referred to as "memory healing," an experiential technique most widely popularized among Christian counselors by David Seamands, in his bestselling books *Healing for Damaged Emotions* (Victor Books, 1981), and *Healing of Memories* (Victor Books, 1985). It involves prayer for healing emotional wounds using the imaginative physical presence of God at the scene of the traumatizing event. Seamands and other authors have given ample scriptural foundation for its practice. I am only one of countless people who have experienced tremendous release from the bondage of the past by God's work through such prayer.

The story told here is not just about me. It is representative of the healing process of thousands who have found the courage to face their pain. Millions of men and women who have been victimized by sexual abuse before they reached the age of eighteen still need to know they did not bring on such assaults by their own behavior, or as a result of some innate "badness." They need to know they are not alone. They need to know there is hope to overcome the pain and to become, at last, who they were designed to be.

CONTENTS

CHAPTER 1

What Was It Like Growing Up?

Looking back, can I explain why I finally admitted my need for help? I guess at first I was focused on fixing my friend Tina's collapsed marriage. It was raging codependency on my part, but I couldn't see it at the time. I was bewildered by my sudden compulsion to suck in every fragment of written wisdom that might be the answer. I only knew that her disaster created such an earthquake in my own life that I couldn't stand not knowing the source of my panic. But I clung to my illusion of control.

By the time Tina's divorce set off that first tremor, my carefully patched self-image had been fractured by a thousand invisible fissures that made up a major fault line. It only took a slight vibration for my self-control to shatter into rubble. From my ruins, Jason's words sounded like a rescue team: "But I'm concerned about you."

Thursday, April 6

Jason recommended starting a journal to jog memories and sort out my feelings. This must be the kind of prescription a therapist writes. Somebody once said that the main purpose of writing is to discover the message inside ourselves. Is there a message? I'll start with the topic of today's therapy session: my earliest significant memory.

Out of the stack of recovery books I read this year, one suggested that early memories are often representative of what childhood as a whole was like. Our brains choose that particular event to hang onto because it sums up the message of a thousand other events we have experienced.

When I read that statement, I was shocked at the force of the picture that suddenly exploded into my mind. The riotous feelings told me it must be important. So this afternoon when Jason asked me what it was like growing up, I told him the story of that disturbing memory.

I can see the kitchen so clearly. The counters and table were piled with clutter in perpetual hopeless disarray. At suppertime we shoved back the encroaching mess to clear enough space to accommodate dishes. The centerpiece was a rarely varying display of the morning's saucer of a half-melted stick of margarine, the sugar bowl encrusted with crystallized spatterings of meals gone by, and dilapidated *Woman's Day* magazines. Likely as not there were dried-out used teabags set on assorted jar lids nestled among a cookbook, a phone directory, leftover dirty glasses, breadcrumbs, and a sprouted sweet potato skewered on toothpicks, its

2

roots filling a quart mayonnaise jar of water, and its vine draggling listlessly toward the light from the dirty window.

It must have been my seventh or eighth birthday. Of course, birthdays at our house passed by unrecognized. No big deal, no party, no present.

But there *was* something different about this birthday. My mother had baked a beautiful angel food cake with whipped cream and strawberries. Actually, she had coincidentally made this cake for dinner, and when reminded that it was my birthday, she called it a birthday cake. But it still made me feel special. Something had been prepared (I told myself) in honor of nobody but *me!*

All through supper I savored the feeling of being valued. I surreptitiously licked my plate clean so none of the perfection of that cake would be contaminated by a stray lump of meat loaf or a limp green bean. Mother never heard of separate dessert plates; they would have made too much work.

I shuddered with anticipation as she cut the cake at last. Without ceremony, she served my big brother Gary first. I was frustrated, but since we had no established birthday etiquette, I was not especially surprised. I contained my growing impatience as she served cake to my older sister, Carla, and my younger half-brother, Will, from Mom's second marriage to Martin. (This must have been before she married Richard, so of course Richie wasn't born yet.) Then she served herself.

But when she sat down and actually began eating her slice of cake, I was so shocked that I burst out, "Mother, I didn't get a piece of my birthday cake!" As she turned to look at me, her eyes hardened into an expression of such cold fury that my disappointment froze into a lump in my throat.

"Don't lie to me to get a second piece of cake!" she snapped. "I gave you the first piece and you ate it already!"

3

Tears filled my eyes as I stared, stunned, down at my perfectly bare plate. I struggled for words of protest, but none would come. The rushing in my ears drowned out Mom's lecture on my poor manners in licking my dish, and I fled from the kitchen in humiliation.

Carla called after me, "You have to come back to help with the dishes!"

The pain behind the tears I sobbed into my pillow that night came back afresh when I first recalled it. Today I thought I could relate that memory calmly to Jason, but the surprising power of the same grief landed again with a hollow thud on my chest. Again, there in the office, I struggled not to cry.

"I think that's significant," I said stiffly. Jason nodded. "My mother didn't believe me . . . she didn't believe *in me*. That's why it stuck in my brain all these years, and why it feels so important now."

But I wasn't prepared for his response. Did I imagine tears in *his* eyes? I never expected him to take it so seriously. "Didn't anybody defend you . . . tell Mom you hadn't had any cake?" he asked. Well, why would they? In our family it was every man for himself. Nobody wasted effort defending anybody else—least of all me. Fact of life.

Then Jason leaned toward me and said softly, "Thank you for trusting me enough to share that. I promise never to do anything to betray your trust."

And why would I be here if I were not willing to trust him? After all, I'm paying for his expertise to help me collate all this stuff I've learned about dysfunctional families from the books. It makes sense to lay it out as quickly as possible so I can be done sooner.

When my time was up, he enclosed my offered hand in both of his bigger hands. He met my eyes without wavering, looking past my protective exterior with makeup all in place, seeing deeper, as if I was transparent. He released his grip as I looked away, unsettled. It must have lasted only a couple of seconds, but for some reason I was unnerved.

Who knows what kind of relationship to expect with a therapist? I've never done this before. To start out as a virtual stranger, and spend the whole time talking about my childhood—personal, painful things—and then for him to look at me that way—with compassion, and caring, as if I meant something to him. But at the same time, I felt exposed, as if he could see the contents of my mind. How'd I get so vulnerable, so fast? Did somebody push the fast-forward button? It's spooky.

Nobody has ever wanted to hear all the feelings crammed down inside me. To have somebody really listen to me now is a new experience. It makes me nervous, but it feels good.

Monday, April 17

So here I am in counseling. My therapist says he sees me on a speeding train, rounding a blind corner with a bridge out just ahead. That he's glad I trusted him enough to begin working with him. He thinks I'm in crisis. Strange. I don't see myself in a crisis.

And he sees the train headed for . . . what? What they used to call a nervous breakdown? Naaah. Jason just doesn't know my capacity for accomplishing a hundred things at once. I'm okay. But this does appear to be an opportunity to figure out those disturbingly familiar scenarios I found in the books I've read, and make my life work better. That's enough value to get from therapy.

Tuesday, April 25

I'd forgotten how much I like to write. I wonder why I haven't been doing this all along.

Jason recommended *Your Inner Child of the Past*, by Hugh Missildine. I had already read it. The inner child concept didn't fit too well with my old idea that, when I graduated from school, I was supposed to be an adult, endowed with the whole set of wisdom and coping skills necessary for life. (No wonder I felt so inadequate . . . my set was missing a whole lot of pieces!)

David Seamands, in *Healing for Damaged Emotions*, compared the inner child to the sapling inside a giant redwood. Years of cell growth and the cumulative effects of environmental conditions develop a tree that surrounds the sapling inside. The outer tree may be tall and old in years, yet the infant organism still lives inside at its core.

Jason says we are going to get to know that child inside me. Judging from the memories we've looked at so far, she is not a happy little girl. As fascinating as this process is, and as much as I am reveling in the attention of being heard as never before, I have some fear about encountering that child.

Many people would call therapy selfish self-pity, I guess. They'd accuse the counselee of wallowing in childhood pain. But I've tried all my life to ignore my background, to pretend it didn't exist. I thought I had forgiven and forgotten, but old memories wouldn't hurt if they were healed. I want to resolve my past and move beyond it to some more effective way of living. Lately, my life isn't working too well.

Saturday, May 6

I guess I never expected therapy to be this tough. All we do is sit in chairs and talk, yet when I leave I feel like I've been in a prize fight. I'm worn out.

Why *is* it so hard? It never bothered me much that I had a difficult childhood. I always knew my family wasn't like the one we used to see on "Leave It to Beaver." My family was "weird." I just accepted the fact that we weren't very happy and tried my best to cope with the present.

But when Jason says, "Tell me about . . .", what comes out isn't merely an intellectual explanation of the facts. I have an overwhelming urge to cry most of the time. Do these startling feelings of—is it grief?—show up just because I'm dealing with specifics? I can't find any other difference.

"What was the atmosphere like at home?" Jason asked. So I told him about frequently waking up in the middle of the night to the sound of Mom and Richard screaming at each other. They got married when I was eight, and I don't remember there ever having been a time they didn't fight. Richard must have been getting ready to go to work . . . he always got up at 3:00 A.M. and left the house at 4:00. There was one time that especially stands out in my memory.

I was startled awake to the same yelling, the volume always turned up to earthshaking. Staring into the darkness, I wished Richard either divorced from us . . . or dead. We'd be better off without him, wouldn't we? He made Mother cry and I was afraid of him. Why *was* I so afraid of him?

Shut up, shut up, shut up, I begged silently. But I knew they would go on and on. *Please God make them stop. I have to go to the bathroom.* I was scared to walk down the hall; they'd see me and I'd be in the middle of the fight. The force of their shouted words whistled through the air and landed like fists delivered hard into the pit of my stomach.

The tension made my swollen bladder ache. *Mom, just don't answer,* I thought. *Let him have the last word and don't argue anymore and he'll go away.* I knew for sure that when I grew up and got married, my husband and I wouldn't fight like that. But Mom never quit. The fights seemed endless.

Then I heard a last explosive curse as a door slammed shut. The windows rattled, then silence settled on the house. I held my breath and strained to listen. Had Richard left for work?

7

I crept into the edge of the hall, ready to dash back into my room if I heard his voice. Mother's muffled sobs came from the living room. Was he gone?

The rush of water in the shower answered my question. Oh, no! He was just *starting* to get ready for work! He always spent at least an hour in there. And a second bathroom was a luxury Mom only dreamed of.

Back in my room, I sank to the floor beside my bed and hugged my knees to my chest, clenching every muscle to keep from wetting myself. My fingertips tingled in sympathy for my bladder. "What am I going to do?" I moaned. I shivered in the cold and pulled my nightgown around my legs. I didn't own a robe.

Carla was in the next bed, either sleeping through it all or pretending to. I rocked myself rhythmically to the throbbing of my abdominal muscles. *Please, please, please, please.*

Once before, I had asked Mom to hurry Richard's shower so I could use the bathroom. She had made me go in while he was still bathing, on the other side of the thin plastic curtain, able to hear every sound I made. It gave me the willies to think about it.

I would *not* do that again. And I couldn't explain why. Mom would just say, "Oh, nonsense. He isn't listening and it doesn't make any difference anyway." She'd be mad if I resisted. Besides, it might start another fight, and I'd be stuck, with no escape. No!

The pain in my abdomen was unbearable, and I was afraid I was going to make a puddle on the linoleum. I pulled my bed pillow onto the floor and sat on top of it. The water was still running, and even after he finished his shower, he would take forever to dress. "What am I going to do?" I whispered again, squeezing my thighs together.

Suddenly there was no decision to make. The pressure in my bladder eased as I lost control. Feeling relief from the pain, I released my knotted muscles and enjoyed emptying myself into the pillow under me. The absence of cramps was such a pleasure that I relaxed into sleepiness.

Except that I had actually wet my bed pillow! That thought snapped me back to alertness. Now what? I could sleep without a pillow tonight, but I couldn't ask Mom to wash it. She'd be furious with me for doing such a nasty, disgusting thing! I'd never hear the end of it. Later she'd tell Richard, too, and they'd join forces against *me*! They'd laugh at me for showing once more how stupid and incompetent I was. Better just to hang my pillow out on the clothesline in the morning. Maybe airing it would be enough. But it would be easier to live with the smell than to let them know.

Wow. Writing that felt just like being there. I can sympathize with that poor child inside me. How hurt she was! There was no way she could win, was there? However she tried to take care of herself, she was always in trouble for what she couldn't help—being a human.

Saturday, May 13, 10:00 P.M.

It's amazing how writing and talking about my childhood bring back events I haven't thought of for more than twenty-five years. Writing about the screaming in the night reminded me of another time I hate to think about. How old was I? Maybe ten.

I woke up and felt so scared about all the yelling that I started crying. My world seemed poised on the brink of a holocaust, and their raging shoved and jostled me ever closer to that fearsome edge. I was powerless to stop the war that threatened to destroy me.

In the twin bed next to mine, Carla spoke up. "What are you crying about? How can you feel sorry for yourself when you think about Jesus dying on the cross? You aren't suffering!" So I shut up. How could I compete with Jesus' pain?

Maybe I shouldn't bother praying any more. My hurt wasn't important enough to bother Him with.

You might have thought, though, when the fight was over and Richard had left for work, that maybe Mom would have come in to comfort us and tell us not to worry about it. She never did. I guess we all pretended that nothing had happened. I made believe I'd been asleep all along and nobody was yelling and we never had this conversation.

Jason said that pretense was one of those family lies. We all made believe everything was okay, ignoring the craziness going on all around us. It's called denial—one of the hallmarks of codependency. I thought codependency only happened in alcoholic families. But I have to admit all the symptoms were there.

Thursday, May 25

Jason and I talked about school today—how my re-entry into college in January "coincidentally" came about when my friend Tina's divorce made me feel so off-balance. I guess I went back to school because I suddenly felt so vulnerable. I mean, if her marriage could dissolve like that, then maybe mine could too, and then what would I do? I was scared. Maybe I overreacted. With my part-time job, the family, and therapy, it's been a tough semester.

I'm only signed up for one class this summer—Psychology 101. It fits with my fascination with understanding what goes on inside people. By now that fascination has driven me to read more than 50 books on the subject. But I've slowed to only one or two books a week.

I was in my element in school. I was appreciated. My teachers loved me. In fact, I was almost always teacher's pet. I never had many friends, though. I always felt different from everyone else. My clothes were one reason why I was different.

By the time she married Richard, Mom had stopped sewing for us, so most of what I wore was either a hand-me-down or from Goodwill. That would have been okay if the garments had been clean and neat. But my clothes always made me ashamed. Hems were out and seams were ripped. When everybody else was wearing wool skirts, sweaters, and knee socks in the winter, I was wearing rumpled cotton dresses, and likely as not, no socks at all. I must have looked like the little match girl.

And I always needed a bath! Weekly baths were the norm in our family. I was a bedwetter, too. Did Mom send me to school smelling of urine? Of course. No wonder I didn't have friends.

I wanted long hair but Mother wouldn't let me grow it out. She said it was too much trouble. I couldn't brush the tangles out, and she didn't help me, so I had rats in my hair all the time. I envied the other girls who looked the way I wanted to look.

Now I wonder whether my teachers loved me because they pitied me! I must have followed them around like a puppy, staying in at recess just to be near them and helping them grade papers after school. How I wished one of them would take me home.

In fact, I worked hard to please anybody who would give me attention. So my report cards, with columns filled with A's, were a source of pride. I'd hand them over to Mother and bask in her approval . . . for all of about thirty seconds.

Later I would hear the comparisons. Gary and Carla got lectures because their grades weren't so great. Gary usually had D's, and Carla got B's and C's. Both of them resented me because Mom used my grades to shame them.

I couldn't help the fact that doing well in school was the only thing that made me feel good about myself. But it cost me what alliance there might have been with my brother and sister. So I guess it should have been no surprise that Carla seemed to prefer to spend time with Gary instead of with me.

I told Jason about the times—at least twice—that I went to school on picture day with curlers in my hair. (Hey, that's the only time it got curled at all!) Since my hair hadn't gotten dry by the time I had to leave for school, Mom told me to ask my teacher to brush it out later. I was humiliated when Mrs. Daniels, my second-grade teacher asked me, before she started to brush it, if I was tender-headed. I wasn't sure what she meant. Nobody had ever asked before.

Jason surprised me when he said, "What you're describing to me is an abusive family. Consistent failure to provide a child with a sense of belonging, personal safety, and self-worth is abuse. They never valued you enough to give you the time it took to brush your hair."

Abuse? I was never hit with a two-by-four. I was spanked with belts and paddles, but does that qualify? I guess Gary was physically abused, though. He got the brunt of Richard's terrible temper. And Martin, the stepfather before Richard, used to be really hard on Gary, too. Maybe that's why Gary was so angry all the time. Still, I had never thought of myself as abused.

But I believe Jason. I know it always made me feel worthless to be treated as though I didn't matter at all. I haven't been a great mother, but I would *never* treat my children like my mother treated me.

Yet Mother and Richard always demanded our respect. Usually in furious shouts. Why would I respect them?

We always heard: "Honor your father and mother" and "Children, obey your parents." I guess they'd never heard: "Fathers, provoke not your children to wrath."

Thursday, June 1

Today I told Jason about a recurring dream I used to have when I was a kid. I was sitting in a car, behind the steering wheel, but I didn't know how to drive. Drive I did, however, up the side of a mountain where the dirt road rose up before me, steeper and steeper, while my heart pounded in my chest and my throat constricted in fear. I heard the crunch and slide of gravel as the tires spun, losing traction. The grade pitched upward alarmingly, and the ground fell away into a rocky canyon of dizzying depth, just inches from the right wheels.

Then the whole mountain was alive, moving, angling the surface of the road upward until the car stalled, yet somehow clung to the side of the vertical cliff. The mountain groaned and shifted as the road ahead suddenly curled above me and doubled back over my head. I gripped the steering wheel. For a moment, the car hung suspended in silence as the roadway now above me pulled away and disappeared. And the car was falling, falling, end over end through space, until I jerked awake with an unborn scream filling my throat. Heart pounding, I stared into the dark.

Thinking about that dream and telling it to Jason gave me the strangest feeling. I'm not sure I understand his response, either, but therapists seem to be deliberately vague sometimes, and after awhile you finally get the idea you're supposed to figure it out for yourself. Did he disagree with the meaning?

I think it means what I now see as my perfectionism. Nothing I ever did was good enough to please my parents, to get their attention and make them love me. What were the standards? All I knew was that I had already failed. I thought I was going to get to the top of the mountain, but the mountain always moved. I could never make it to the top. So I kept trying harder.

When I shared that theory with Jason, he nodded and then thought for a while. "That might fit," he said. "Your perfectionism is a direct result of the absence of support and approval in your family. I don't spend a great deal of time on

13

interpretation of dreams, and you may be the best person to tell me what your dream means. But perhaps we'll understand more in the context of other scenes we look at as we go on."

So I still don't get it. Have I missed something? File it under interesting, unresolved, and very disturbing.

Friday, June 9

Jason asked me yesterday whether I liked being a girl when I was a kid. So I told him, "Yeah. I always knew I didn't want to be a boy! So a girl is the only other option."

Strange. I just thought about the fact that Grandma used to order pajamas from the catalog every year for our Christmas. They must have gotten the orders wrong, because time and time again, when my sister and I opened the packages on Christmas morning, we found boy's ski pajamas inside. The ones that are supposed to look like a football jersey. With a fly in the front, of course. So that's what we wore.

If my brothers' pajamas had turned out to be yellow flannel with rosebuds, Grandma would have found a way to exchange them in time for Christmas. I guess she thought it was okay for a girl to wear a boy's style. Girls didn't matter so much. But I always wished for flannel and rosebuds. And lace.

Come to think of it, I don't have any warm memories of happy Christmases past. As a matter of fact, I can't find any warm childhood memories of *anything* in our family. What happened to the history I thought I had?

My whole history turns out to be fiction. Everything I ever told myself about the people I grew up with was a lie. The "family" I imagined I had was a defense mechanism I created so I didn't have to face the fact that nobody ever cared about me. If I've got a face only a mother could love, and Mother

14

doesn't love it, doesn't that say I'm not worth loving? I couldn't admit the truth.

Do all therapists know exactly the right questions to ask to bring up all this uncomfortable stuff? It's uncanny. And I can't seem to find the "off" switch once Jason's question or comment sets my mental gears in motion.

One comment he made came at me out of the blue. He said, "You may find that this work you are doing has the effect of allowing you increased intimacy with your husband."

What? Who brought up the subject of sex? Certainly not me. I didn't answer him. I was too astonished to reply.

Wednesday, June 21, 1:30 A.M.

What is my problem? I keep waking up in the middle of the night with my brain in high gear. Reading usually puts me back to sleep eventually, but tonight I can't seem to focus on a book. So I pull out the notebook. I'm *not* excited to be writing. Oh, please. I just want to sleep.

Okay, here goes. One of the things Jason asked me during the last visit was "How did you cope when you were a little girl?" That's easy. I read books. I escaped into the world of fiction where moms serve milk and cookies and say, "How was your day, dear?" I climbed my tree in the front yard and, sitting on a branch among the leaves, I read everything I could get my hands on. I became the character inside those pages, and I didn't come out until I couldn't pretend any longer that I didn't hear them yelling my name.

I also ate. Food was the only friend I had at home. So from the age of nine or ten, there was the added embarrassment of being fat. The remarks people made. The name-calling.

My family had plenty of ammunition to use against me. "Judy's always got her nose in a book or she's daydreaming. Hasn't got a speck of common sense. Fat. Ugly. Lazy. Clumsy."

15

Mom pointedly avoided the word stupid. She never called me that exactly. But it was the message I always read in her eyes.

What chance did I have to be normal? They told me how inadequate I was from the time I could walk! For a child to be shamed like that is the loneliest feeling in the world.

I suddenly have a picture—a very clear picture—of that child still living inside me. She is a child without a friend in the world. A child with no one who would take her side. A child who tried so hard to be loved, to be accepted, to be good. But it's never been enough. I can see this inner child huddled into a ball in the corner, holding herself because nobody else will hold her. And crying because she is so alone.

Some of the books talk about parenting that inner child, about learning to comfort her. But how do you do that? She needs to be held. She needs to be told that somebody cares whether she lives or dies. She needs somebody to love her.

She is *me,* only younger: *judy.* And I'm the only one she's got. I'm the only one who knows how much she hurts. So I guess I'm the one who has to put down the pencil and hold her. And listen to her. Tell her I accept her. I know how desperately she always tried. I won't be one of the ones who shame her anymore. I won't call her names anymore. I'll learn to love her.

Wednesday, June 21, 10:00 A.M.

Well, I finally got back to bed about 4:00 A.M. I don't quite know how to explain last night. Maybe I can't.

After I stopped writing, I turned out the lamp and curled up on the couch, clutching a pillow on my lap. I was that little girl again and yet, at the same time, I was the adult who wanted more than anything to comfort her. I held her and rocked her and wept with her as she poured out her loneliness and loss and longing for everything she never had. We cried for two hours until we had both spent all our energy in that storm of grief.

I am awed at having touched the core of hurt in the sad little girl I used to be . . . and still carry inside me. How I have minimized her pain for all these years! I joined the team of people who shamed her, abused her, and made her feel less than nothing.

But no more. I respect her suffering. It was real. She deserves to be honored for surviving such a wasteland.

CHAPTER 2

Past Halfway?

Rereading my journal makes me ache even now, after these wounds have been healed. I wanted so desperately to be airlifted out of the suffering therapy brought to the surface.

Even before I recognized her voice, my inner child was crying out to be heard and understood. I was puzzled by exclamations coming from my mouth or my pen that didn't fit my adult, polished facade. Her vocabulary was not my own. She spoke in the language of a child.

Thursday, June 29, 9:00 P.M.

After only fourteen counseling hours, I think my therapist knows me better than I know myself. He even knows my *family* better than they know themselves.

Today I shared with Jason a memory that must be my earliest. It hasn't come to mind before, but it reminded me what a creep my brother Gary is.

When I was two, Mom went to the store and left Gary in charge of Carla and me. So Gary, at six years old, was baby-sitting. I asked him for a drink of water, since I couldn't reach the faucet. He refused and kept on refusing, and my thirst grew into a panic. He taunted me for whining.

Finally, tired of my insistence, he grabbed an empty Coke bottle off the kitchen table and thrust it at me. "Here!" he said with a smirk. "Just spit into this bottle, and then drink it!" He laughed hysterically at his own wit.

I finished with a comment about Gary's character as an adult and shifted to a new topic of conversation, but Jason stopped me short and backed me up to explain. Gary has been in prison several times, has married and divorced three times, once to a stripper. He used to sell drugs, and who knows what else. Jason said, "You never told me that!" Well, we've covered a lot of ground. I couldn't tell him everything. We haven't concentrated on my brother much. I haven't seen him in years, thank goodness.

It was another productive session. Little pieces keep falling into place. The puzzle is beginning to make more sense. Coincidentally, my Psych class in summer school has confirmed so much about how lessons instilled in childhood affect us.

But I was startled to hear the question, "How does it feel to look back over your shoulder and see the crest of the hill behind you?"

"You think I'm past halfway?"

"Unless something else important shows up," he replied.

Wow! That's a surprise. Of course I had started counseling thinking I was just going to make sense of all the information I'd already gotten from books. But for Jason to suggest that I might actually be finishing therapy made me feel as though I wasn't quite ready to call it quits yet. I was just getting comfortable. But, he's the expert.

Monday, July 3, 3:00 P.M.

I feel as though someone has just dropped an anvil on my chest, and I can't explain why. This morning in Psych 101 we began talking about antisocial personalities. Not the kind of people you want to hang out with. Criminals. I sat at my desk staring at my textbook oblivious to the professor for a long time because what kept shouting out at me was that I *know* a person like that. Every characteristic in the book described my brother Gary. It was as if the authors knew him personally. They didn't like him, either.

I was so upset, it's a wonder I didn't have an accident driving home. My heart was pounding and my throat felt like a chunk of granite was stuck in it. Running through my head was this recycling tape whispering, *My brother is a criminal. And my brother molested me!* Now where did that come from? And why do I feel like death? I cannot make sense of this.

If you had asked me directly if I had been molested as a child, I would always have answered yes. It wasn't as if I had forgotten it. But it never mattered. It didn't mean anything. Why does it feel now as if it meant *everything*?

21

Thank God, my husband has the day off today, because I am ill. I can't cope with the girls. I will let David be the good father today. I feel paralyzed, unable to do anything but indulge myself in a crying jag. What *is* the matter with me?

I told David about this feeling. "I hope you don't have any major expectations of me today, because I can't accomplish anything. I'm going to be worthless."

"I don't have any expectations of you *at all* for the duration of your therapy," he answered.

Bless him. He's been taking my stuff almost as seriously as I have. Well, not quite. Seeing how compulsively I'm going at therapy (still reading books the way I can eat chocolate chip cookies), that's pretty seriously. But suddenly it looks as though the intensity has mushroomed.

Jason will help me make sense of this. At least I have my weekly appointment in two days. I hope I can last that long.

Thursday, July 6, 11:30 P.M.

Well, I dumped it on Jason this afternoon. He could see I was suffering when he first laid eyes on me. "Are you struggling?" he asked, as I pantomimed a person choking to death, hands clutching throat, tongue extended, eyes rolled back. That's exactly how I felt.

"Yes!"

And then he waited. He just waited for me to spit it out. *Does he know how hard this is? Yeah, I think he does.*

So I haltingly told him about Psychology class, that my brother is an antisocial personality . . . and that he molested me.

"I thought so," he said gently.

I moaned inwardly. "What . . . am I wearing a sign?"

"No, Judy. No. I couldn't be sure. But you were denied the right to protect yourself from the very first. If there was anyone around you, within the family or without, who was looking to release their own frustrations by acting out sexually, what defenses did you have?"

None. "But," I protected, "this memory has been sitting on an obscure shelf in the back of my mind, labeled 'Doesn't matter' for all my life. Why do I feel this way *now?* It isn't as if he raped me. It was *only* touching!"

The sympathy in his eyes nearly sent me over the edge. But I held back my tears.

"The reason you feel this way is because it *is* important. He had no right to do what he did. He stole from you your right to protect yourself. If you aren't allowed to be in control of your own body, then you have been violated. He committed a criminal act against you and, if it had happened today, he would very likely be put in prison for it." Then Jason said, "Tell me about your brother."

I don't want to talk about Gary! I drew a breath. "My brother is a snake," I said. Jason nodded. "He was only four years older, but he was so different! I was always afraid of him. He had an explosive temper. He gave me Indian burns on my arms, and he pinched my nipples. He had an interesting collection under his bed. Dirty magazines, of course. He also had an eight-foot leather bullwhip and a machete and a switchblade knife. Violent things."

I told him how Gary held my head under water, nearly drowning me in the motel pool when I was four, when Mom had left us alone. I told him about the time I wanted my brother to play with me on the seesaw and he kept teasing me, keeping my end too high for me to reach. Then he "changed his mind" and sent my end of the heavy plank crashing down on my head. I had a black eye for two weeks. I was five years old.

I told Jason how I had never learned to ride a bicycle because Gary was the person Mom designated to teach me on the "family" bicycle (I never had one of my own). After trying for a long time to balance on this boy's-style bike, far too large for me, I gave up rather than continue to listen to Gary's taunts and insults. I couldn't stand to hear any more of his ridicule. Afterward, it became a family joke that Judy couldn't even ride a bicycle. Klutz!

When Gary was eleven, the police came to our house after one of the little girls in the neighborhood reported him for molesting her. He had to go in for mandatory counseling for a while, and Mom was pretty upset, but it blew over. So Mom knew what Gary was like.

With the exception of Dennis, the older kid next door that he looked up to, Gary hung out with friends who were just as mean as he was, hoodlums who ditched school and were in trouble with the police. He carried out the same profile as an adult.

"But my brother was that way because of the way *he* had been abused!" I told Jason. "He was six when our real father, Jack, divorced Mom. I was too little to remember, but Gary remembered Jack's beatings. After that, she was married to Martin for two years, and Martin was hard on Gary, too. Gary was always in trouble, and he got hit a lot. And then Richard! He called Gary 'stonehead' and 'ironhead.' He really hated Gary. Gary had it rough."

Jason's response silenced me. "I think you've cut your brother enough slack," he said. "He was still responsible for hurting an innocent child."

I didn't have a reply to that. Still, it was a relief that my therapist was taking me so seriously.

Then came the moment I feared. "You know that we need to talk about this. Or did you think that once you had told me it happened, you could forget it?"

I took a deep breath. "No. Now that it's out, I can't stuff it back into the box it came from. It won't fit anymore. I can't forget it." I felt myself tensing as if anticipating a collision.

"How old were you?" Jason asked.

"Nine? I don't know!"

"Can you tell me what happened?" he probed very gently.

Why, why ,why, why do I have to go through this, to say the words? I thought. Another ragged breath. My throat hurt.

"I remember once—coming back from Gary's room late at night. I passed Carla in the hallway. She put out her hand to touch my waist, to see if I was wearing underwear under my nightgown. I wasn't." I stared hard at my shoes, intermittently holding my breath and forcing myself to exhale. "The look she gave me was as if to beg me, 'Oh, don't let him do that!' She knew, but she didn't say the words. I guess that meant Gary molested her too."

"Is there anything else?"

"The only other time I can remember," I started slowly, "was when I was sitting on the couch in the living room and nobody else was home. Gary came and sat beside me and put his hand under my dress . . ." I stopped.

Jason waited. Finally he said, "And he stimulated you?"

I must have winced. I wonder what other reflex movement I made because I felt as if I had been slapped. Finally I whispered, "Yes," and closed my eyes.

I wanted to scream. I wanted to leap out of the chair and hide in the corner. Or run. I wanted to be anywhere but there. But this horrible feeling was not going to go away on its own. I felt as though somebody had died and I had to talk to someone about it. Jason, my therapist, was my only hope of getting past this nightmare. Even if it meant telling him all this awful stuff about myself. Telling a *man!*

Mercifully, he let me off the hook. He didn't make me say any more. When he began to speak, I hung on his words. I wanted to hear *something* that would make the pain go away. *Does he have a magic wand? I hope so.*

25

But what he said was, "Jesus has been longing for you to bring this into the light, so He can heal it. You've been in bondage to the sin that was committed against you for so many years."

I want so much to believe what Jason said. For him to talk about God *healing* me makes me wish for a miracle, but I don't have any confidence in that. The age of miracles was to establish the church, wasn't it? God doesn't do that stuff anymore. Does He? So where does that leave me now? Hurting. Alone.

When my time was up, I had the impulse to throw a tantrum, cling to his ankles, beg him not to make me go back out there alone. Or maybe that was *judy's* impulse. But because I didn't want to embarrass myself, I resisted.

Jason must have observed that I was still upset, though. After thanking me for trusting him with this memory, he made a point of saying how *he* trusted *me* to be okay after I went out the door. Nice. But who's going to pick me up off the floor?

I *did* ask if I could have sessions twice a week just until I get through this issue. I can't stand to wait a whole week. I am *so* thankful he said yes.

As we were going out the door, I asked, "Do you still think I'm past halfway?"

And I wasn't too surprised when he replied, "Maybe not. But we'll take it a little at a time."

I stopped on the way home (with my everything's-in-control mask in place) and bought chocolate cupcakes. Sugar—my drug of choice. I stuffed them in as fast as possible. It settled my shakes a little. But I was still quaking inside. I begin to see the attraction in getting drunk. Oblivion.

Friday, July 7, 3:00 P.M.

Yesterday Jason said, "If there was anyone, within the family or without, who was looking to release his own frustrations by acting out sexually . . ." He was confirming my revelation about Gary.

But it also made me think about Leo. Leo wasn't in the family. He dated my mother after her second divorce, before she married Richard. When I was five years old, Leo took me into my mother's bedroom—and showed me his penis. Maybe I *was* wearing a sign, even then. But it doesn't feel important. It's—numb.

What makes one incident seem trivial and the other—so dreadfully heavy? I don't know.

I feel as if I'm in mourning.

Saturday, July 8, 2:30 A.M.

My brain will not let me sleep. I am cringing at having to *think*, let alone *write down* the dream I had as a teenager. I remembered it yesterday afternoon, out of the blue. I can't get rid of it. The image is like a hamster running on one of those little wire wheels, around and around in my head. I can't make it stop. I *hate* this, but here it is:

I was recycling the mental "tape" of Thursday's therapy session and I heard again what I had said to Jason: "My brother is a *snake*." Oh, no! There is no more obvious a phallic symbol than a snake. You don't have to be a psychologist to know that snake equals penis. And with that thought came the image of that dream (*was* it a dream?) from years ago.

In that old dream I was lying naked on a bed. I was frozen, petrified with fear, paralyzed, although there was nothing physically holding me down. At the foot of the bed between my feet was an enormous snake, coiled as if to strike. I watched in horror as the snake lifted itself, uncoiled, and, flicking its tongue, glided slowly, silently toward me. Closer

27

and closer it came, until it entered my vagina. I wanted to scream, but no sound came out. And here the memory ends.

Obviously I'm no expert, but I have read enough to know that my "dream" has to mean that there was intercourse. And my guts tell me that's what happened, too. Somehow I *know* and can't pretend otherwise. My hand is shaking as I write this. My whole body is shaking.

Just because I don't remember actual penetration doesn't mean it didn't happen. Although I've always been dubious, repression of memory is said to be very common in people from traumatic backgrounds. Surely this qualifies as trauma.

Knowing the violent kind of person Gary was, and how afraid of him I was, I could not have stopped him from doing anything he wanted. He would not have stopped himself, either. Touching would not have been enough. Intercourse. At nine years old. For how many years? He didn't leave home till I was fourteen. *God help me.*

Saturday, July 8, 11:30 P.M.

You'd think I wouldn't even bother trying to go to sleep when I've been reading and thinking about incest all day. I can't *stop* thinking about it. Writing it down seems to help. It stills the hamster wheel. So I'll spit it out.

In high school I had the reputation of some cross between "brain" and "pure as the driven snow"—a regular Goody Two-Shoes. Eyes widened in shock the few times anybody ever heard me say a bad word.

David was my second steady boyfriend. We dated for a long time before we crossed the line between "making out" and "heavy petting." In my mind I always made a very big point of the fact that we never "went all the way" before we got married. So technically I was a virgin on my wedding night. Or so I thought.

But that doesn't jibe with the first time David and I got very carried away and I didn't stop him.... (It has taken me an hour to write this sentence and I still can't make the words go down on paper.) When our heads had cleared, David asked me, "How did you lose your hymen?"

I jerked bolt upright and stared at him in shock. "Isn't it *there*?" I asked, my voice shriller than I intended. I was at a loss. A little scrap of flesh that meant the difference between being a good girl or a bad girl was mysteriously missing, and I had no idea why. David accepted my stammered speculation that I must have "lost it" during physical exercise without knowing it. *Me*, a bookworm since the first grade!

I haven't thought about that conversation since that night. But the mystery is certainly solved by knowing that there was intercourse with my brother. *I want to throw up.* If repressed memories are real, then surely intercourse is one memory I would want to repress. More likely there's a major series of memories I would have repressed, rather than let them make me crazy.

Jason says the resurfacing of repressed memories is called flashback, and that more is understood about it because of the work done with Vietnam vets. I'm scared to death to even think about reliving those times in flashback. I don't want to go back there again. I don't *want* to know what happened. I am so afraid to look at what is down inside me. *I do not want to remember!*

I started to write that this feeling I have is guilt, but Jason explained the difference between guilt and shame a few weeks ago. Guilt is when I make a mistake. Shame is when I carry the feeling that I *am* a mistake. And shame is what I am feeling now. *I am bad. How could I have done that? With my brother! How could I?*

I still have to make it through this weekend. My next session on Tuesday afternoon seems so far away.

29

Tuesday, July 11, 4:00 P.M.

This afternoon I tried to disregard my shaking hands and queasy stomach as I gathered my courage and told Jason the snake dream. "I don't think I could have had that dream without knowing there was intercourse." He nodded. Then a new thought occurred to me. "Except that it was rape, wasn't it?"

"Yes. It was."

"Carla wouldn't agree it was rape. She'd say, 'You weren't screaming, were you?'" I covered my mouth with my hand and stared hard at my shoes.

"You were screaming," Jason said firmly.

Everything in me agrees with that. I have wanted to scream and keep on screaming ever since this whole topic came up. But my screams have all been silent ones.

I blew my nose. "Do you know where tears go when they don't come out your eyes?" Jason asked.

So, he sees through my strong, self-possessed exterior.

"Yes," I said, focusing intently on the Kleenex I was crumpling in my fist. "They drain into your nose." I blew again. There's nothing to hide behind in therapy.

More and more I've had the feeling that Jason's not in control here. And obviously I'm not in control. I've never felt so out-of-control in my life. "I feel as though you and I are just standing on the sidelines," I told him, "and God is the one directing this therapy."

"Did you just realize that?" Like maybe everybody's therapy is this way.

"Jason, it hurts!" I said to him as we stood at the end of the session.

He nodded soberly. "I won't pretend to know how much it hurts, Judy, but I'm praying for you."

No instant cure, I guess. Talking about it helped a lot, but I still feel like a shotgun has blasted a hole in my guts. And oddly, I find myself walking gingerly, hunched a little, holding my right hand pressed against my midsection. Like I'm keeping my liver and intestines from falling out onto the floor. It's a reflex, but even being aware of it, I am still holding myself. There is the tiniest bit of comfort in it. And I'll take any comfort I can get.

It's all I can do to get through each day. I feel so helpless and afraid and sad all the time. I don't know what to tell my children. They're overdosing on videotapes while I hole up in the bedroom and cry. I'm not coping with any domestic responsibilities right now. I'm not cleaning house or cooking.

But I'm still reading voraciously. Maybe I'm looking for the answer in the books. I haven't found it yet.

Wednesday, July 19, 11:00 A.M.

My inner child—the nine-year-old *judy* inside me—has been stuck in the pain and fear of those awful scenes for more than twenty-five years. My sadness for her losses jumps out at me unexpectedly and overwhelms me. I'm falling apart.

People at church are wondering what my problem is. They must think I'm crazy. Maybe I am. I cry at the drop of a hat. In fact, I seem to be weeping half my waking hours. And I can't hold an ordinary conversation with anybody. My mind is on a single track, and I can't seem to focus on anything else.

They would understand if I could tell them someone in my family died. People know about that kind of grief. But this is grief, too. First of all, I have to face the fact that the family I always imagined I had was a cardboard construction inside my head. That cardboard family is now in a bus plunging off a cliff. So someone *has* died.

And now that the topic of incest has surfaced, I have a whole new magnitude of grief for the losses of the child I was. I lost my innocence. I lost my virginity to someone who used me for his own selfish needs and threw me away. He never gave a thought to the value of what he stole from me. I lost the wonder of first discovering sexuality with my husband. I grieve those losses.

I need to know there is *somebody* who knows what I'm going through and who is sympathetic toward me. I need somebody to support me, to offer to take my kids for the afternoon once in awhile, or just to make eye contact with me and give me a hug. I feel so alone.

So I enlisted David's support, and I have picked out a few people to tell about my therapy. I told them I've discovered repressed memories that I was sexually abused in childhood. One person said incredulously, "You mean you *forgot?*" Maybe I shouldn't have chosen *her* to tell. Not helpful.

I've also talked to Carla on the phone a whole lot. My long distance bills will be awful. She listens to me, but I have the feeling she'd rather change the subject. And on the topic of Gary, she said, "But I never thought of him as malicious!" Are we talking about the same person?

I think Jason had some reservations about my telling people. Maybe he didn't mean to let me see that, and he didn't make a big deal about it, but he did say that some of those people might not be safe to share with.

But I have to tell *somebody!* I look like death warmed over, and I feel worse. I have to know somebody cares and doesn't think I'm just being weird. Not that I'm announcing it in Sunday school class. But surely one of these friends that have been family to me for the last twelve years will come through and support me. *Please?*

I can't continue to live like this for long. I can't stand it. The thought of my abuse never leaves my brain from morning to night! I need to find a way to forgive my brother for what he did. God commands me to forgive. Forgiveness will disconnect me from the abuse, won't it? Maybe that will make the pain go away. I wonder why Jason hasn't raised the issue of forgiveness already.

CHAPTER 3

Just Say No!
How Do You Do That?⎯⎯⎯⎯⎯

In the midst of such detailed self-examination, all the basic assumptions of my identity had shifted. Incest was on my heart and mind every waking moment. I felt soiled and used.

Once I asked David what he had seen in me that attracted him when we met. He thought seriously for a minute and answered, "Purity". I dissolved into tears of grief for that lost illusion, but he said, "That purity was there. It still is." Could it have been that the abuse never touched the heart of who I really am?

Tuesday, July 25, 10:30 P.M.

I'm still in shock from my therapy session this afternoon. We talked about boundaries—that invisible bubble of personal space around us that protects us from unwanted intrusion. Like being able to protect myself from my brother. Or not being able to. The little "exercise" we did brought me face to face with my inability to say no.

Jason sat facing me, his chair pulled close to mine. Holding his hands up in front of him, he asked me to place my hands against his and to close my eyes. Scary already. Then he said, "I promise you that I won't touch you anywhere but your palms. I'm going to push against your hands. I want you to resist the pressure and tell me to stop whenever you want."

It sounded simple. So why was my heart beating so hard? I *knew* I was sitting in a counselor's office, at one o'clock in the afternoon, as an adult. But suddenly I felt like a frightened nine-year-old. I was *back there* again.

And it was a nine-year-old voice I heard coming from my lips. "*Stop!*" the voice pleaded. But he kept on pressing gently against my hands. "*Stop!*" I said again and again. "*Don't!*" But he didn't stop. I felt so helpless. If the words wouldn't stop him, what was I supposed to do? I was nearly in tears before Jason finally told me to open my eyes.

As I slowly pried my lids apart, he released the pressure against my hands. I gasped as I saw that my hands had been pushed all the way back, even with my shoulders. I had been so afraid, yet I hadn't physically resisted him at all!

"I believe little Judy wanted to stop what happened to her," Jason said. "She tried to say no, over and over again.

36

But no one was listening. They taught her that resistance was useless. She never had an opportunity to protect herself. She was helpless and innocent, and what happened to her wasn't her fault. There is nothing . . . nothing that will make me believe she was *bad*."

It's going to take me awhile to assimilate this. I'm still shaking.

Wednesday, July 26, 2:00 A.M.

There seems to be an alarm that goes off in my head at 1:30 A.M.! Night after night I wake up at about this time. So here I am with my notebook and pencil, after resisting the idea of writing, but knowing that only writing will still the voices in my head.

I wish I had a nickel for each of the tears I've shed this year. Yet now, knowing it was the specter of incest hiding in the forgotten corners of my mind, I wonder how many tears were forced inside because I couldn't speak the pain of what was happening to me. My mother didn't believe me. I learned early that she didn't want to hear what I had to say.

What would my inner child have said if she could have given voice to her fear? *judy* was comforted by the connection we made when I wept with her . . . when I first began to see how hurt she was. Maybe now she feels safe enough to talk to me.

Are you with me now, *judy*? I'd like to listen if you could tell me what you're feeling.

Will you believe me? Nobody's ever believed me all my life. Why would it be different now?

Because you're part of me. I can see at last how much you were hurt, how hard you tried to be good. I promise not to shame you. It wasn't your fault. Were you afraid?

I was scared to be with Gary. He always did such bad things. He lied to Mama all the time, but she believed him. I could tell the truth and still be accused of lying and get punished for what I didn't do. Was there something special about boys that made them more important than girls? There must have been another set of rules, because Mama always took his side. She always defended him . . . the way I wanted her to defend me. She loved him. How could I tell her what he was doing to me?

But didn't she love you, too? You were her daughter.

I needed her to love me. But I could never feel it. I felt as if some giant vacuum had sucked all the love out of the universe. I needed someone to love me, but I was all alone. Gary said he loved me . . . when he wanted to touch me.

But did he really?

No, it was another one of his lies. Even so, I wanted so much to believe he did . . . I kept hoping. Nobody else even said the words to me.

And then there were those shivery feelings I got whenever he put his hands on me. It must be wrong to have those feelings. He was being bad and he made me bad, too. I was afraid and ashamed, but excited and pleased at the same time. Is that what love feels like?

No. Love is supposed to feel good. It doesn't make you ashamed. You've had a lot of confusing messages about the sexual feelings you couldn't help having. You weren't bad for having sexual feelings. Those feelings happen automatically. He took advantage of you. He confused you.

I was confused! He made me want those good feelings, and then I saw how dirty and nasty it all was, but I couldn't help myself. I couldn't stop him and I couldn't stop myself, and I felt dirtier and dirtier. So I hated myself for letting it happen.

I didn't know how to say no. Nobody ever ever ever listened when I said stop, anyway. And Gary was so much stronger than me . . . even if I tried to stop him, he could hurt me. And he would! I didn't want to hurt anymore! I've been hurting since I was so little. Couldn't I have one good feeling in my life? I didn't know what to

*do. And there was nobody to help me figure it out. They would all
know I was bad because I didn't stop him.*

Jason doesn't think you're bad. He said you were innocent
and defenseless. He says Gary was responsible for taking
advantage of you and hurting you. And I think he's right.

Nobody ever gave you the right to say no. Mom never let
you disagree with anything she said. We were never allowed
to express an opinion. Richard exploded into a rage if you
talked back to him. No didn't mean anything in our house,
except to get you in trouble.

Jason's going to help us figure it out. He says God wants
to heal it. I'm not sure about that, but I trust Jason. He says
it's not going to feel so awful forever.

And I believe in you. I'm going to find a way to stop your
hurting and learn how to take care of you. So maybe you can
sleep now. Both of us can rest.

Saturday, July 29, 12:45 A.M.

Sleep eludes me again. I have been staring at this blank
sheet of paper for the past hour. Stalling.

Is it the coward's way out to write what I'm afraid to say
and give it to Jason to read? I'm afraid to say it to his face. He
tells me it's okay to feel my feelings now, and what I feel is
fear. Cowardice or not, I will force my hand to write.

Okay. Deep breath. I've decided it doesn't make any sense
to go to the enormous effort this process has taken without
clearing up every possibility of a hang-up. And since I seem
to have been stalling even on paper, maybe this *is* a hang-up.

Of course it's a hang-up! The topic is *sex*.

But if I make sexuality an off-limits subject for discussion
in therapy, that leaves me open for a big blind spot where I
have the most concern for being healthy. Because the central
hurt in my childhood has been sexual, there probably *is* some
scarring there.

Is it okay to talk about sex with a therapist? I don't know what the rules are! But it is my *counselor* who raised the issue in the first place, so I think he's giving me permission to say whatever is on my mind. Now if my brain will just give my hand permission to put it down on paper. *Write!*

Jason said the most common response to childhood sexual abuse is adult sexual dysfunction. To which I replied, "But I don't consider myself sexually dysfunctional!"

"I'm glad for you."

Hearing that felt strange. I know in theory women are *supposed* to have sexual pleasure, just like men. But to have a Christian counselor, as an authority figure, give me his stamp of approval for me to enjoy sex is something else again. It's still *bad* to *judy*.

Who am I kidding? Get real. Yes, I am orgasmic. (Forming those letters on paper is like hearing fingernails on a chalkboard ... I *hate* it! But I can't go the rest of my life with these questions thumping around in my head. I need to be able to sleep sometime.) I *do* reach orgasm. *But ...*

I have read enough books to know that my own experience of getting to the point of orgasm isn't as simple as the books set forth as "normal" (if there is such a thing). Is there a reason I have such a hard time concentrating on what's going on in bed with my husband? Why do I suddenly think of what to make for dinner the next day, or whether I forgot to enter the last check I wrote, or anything else except sex?

So the whole process of sex is frustrating. It takes forever, and much of the time it doesn't seem worth it. Is this the same kind of sex Eve experienced with Adam in the Garden of Eden? I think not.

And some of my wires are disconnected. You mean it's supposed to feel good when my husband ... well, I don't feel much of anything. Speaking of wires, Jason said that when a child is sexualized before she is emotionally and physically

to the girl to defend her own virtue because boys certainly had no motivation or responsibility to preserve it for her.

Girls were the ones with the power to arouse boys, to tease them, and to say yes or no to them. Girls had the rational control in a clinch. If a girl didn't have control, she would get a *reputation* for going too far and, after that, any boy she went out with would have an assumed right to go to the limits she had established. Then he would push to extend those boundaries so he could "go all the way." It was expected!

Her reputation was her fault because she hadn't been strong enough to stop a steamroller. She knew he was a steamroller when she went out with him, didn't she? Boys never got a reputation. They were only fulfilling the culturally indulged expectation to sow their wild oats.

What I rarely heard addressed was that a girl had a sex drive, too, and that very probably she would not feel rational about being in control of heavy petting on dates. Failing to hit the brakes on a date made her bad, for which she would be punished—by the reputation and the fear of, or even the reality of pregnancy.

Because the consequences of pregnancy affected her so much more than him, the responsibility for the use of birth control still rested on her. Meanwhile, the boy (wham bam not even a thank-you ma'am) had faded into the sunset while she was left frustrated, alone, and shamed. Shamed, because she was bad.

She wasn't expected to be orgasmic, anyway. He was too wrapped up in his own drive toward ejaculation to consider her pleasure, even if he imagined she needed any. Her goal was to be loved. Fat chance of that!

It's no wonder a girl from a dysfunctional, shaming, addictive family is so likely to end up as an unwed mother. Statistics bear that out. She's trying desperately to find somebody who will love her the way she has never felt loved, in the only way she has ever seen affection expressed. She was set up to be in that bind.

When you put together all these cultural puzzle pieces, they form an interesting picture: God is a *male* who designed sex for the propagation of the race (making babies for which women are responsible) and as a setup for women—to benefit men. "Wives submit to your own husbands" (Eph. 5:22, NKJV).

Men are practically guaranteed sexual release. Okay, Jason would remind me of all the men who suffer from impotence. Spare me. I don't want to hear about it.

Women deny men their "rights" to sex, so they are labeled a whole long list of bad names. Or, women allow sex in the futile hope of achieving intimacy, love, and financial support. Which makes women pretty stupid, huh?

If a woman *does* enjoy sex, she pays the price of guilt—for not exercising control, for being bad, and for getting something she doesn't deserve. The system isn't designed for her pleasure. It's a pretty nasty trick for God to play on women. Women have all of the guilt, all of the responsibility, and all of the work in cleaning up the mess sex makes in people's lives. Sex is a cruel joke on women, intended to make them more powerless than ever!

If I had been God, I would have designed the same scenario, except with the roles reversed. Now *there* would be the way to get even with men for being all the evil things I perceived them to be!

Let *men* go through the mess and pain of periods every month, become the subject of snickering and humiliating jokes for something they never asked for! Let *men* carry a growing baby inside their bodies for all those months . . . a total invasion of their whole being! And then let *men* deliver that child in the midst of pain, only to rise from the delivery

table to subordinate their needs to the demands of a screaming infant.

Let *men* change the dirty diapers, wipe the snotty noses,
clean up the vomit when it's sick, comfort it when it's hurt,
and then carry all the guilt when that child turns out wrong.
That's the lot of women. Enslavement to the responsibilities
men deny.

Men are holding all the cards, and we are at their mercy.
When did I ever see a man who wouldn't have taken advantage of me? I learned those lessons well when I was a child.

Add to this the list of codependent rules in my family. My
opinions weren't valid, and I had no permission to express
them. That pretty effectively took away my ability to say no
to sex: I was damned if I did and damned if I didn't. There
was no way to protect my damaged virtue.

I was brainwashed to be in subjugation to men. And if I
were to be no more than a possession to a man, when I
knew men to be so evil, then my own value plummeted.
Self-esteem? What's that? Why would I have any hope but
resignation to the master plan? Submit to God and submit
to my husband.

My "submission" to David, therefore, always had a germ
of anarchy inside it. There was always a dagger up my sleeve.
He *seemed* so much different from the other men I had known,
but when I looked hard enough, I could see the telltale signs
that fulfilled my expectations of him. Sometimes it took a
little sabotage to bring out those characteristics, but then I
expected them to be there all along, didn't I?

As I write this, I suddenly see how orgasm equals a total
giving over of control of my body to a man . . . who already
has almost total control over my life. Can't I withhold at least
that?

I don't think I ever experienced orgasm with Gary, but
what an awful thing it must have been if I had! What a nasty

smirk he must have had on his face in the midst of it, and what shame I had to have felt for losing control like that. How I hated him for putting me in such a bind that I had to hate myself. I was responsible because men are not responsible!

(Long pause while my blood pressure returns to normal.)

I am stunned. It's obvious I have a deep distrust, even hatred, for men. What's so amazing is that I've always considered myself very comfortable with men. I have men friends. I trust my husband. Where was all this sewage lurking? My inner child was compelled to submerge it totally just to survive in an evil male world, created by a sadistic male God. I cry for her despair.

Saturday, August 12, 2:00 A.M.

Another memory has taken me by surprise. I woke up with an old picture in my head that drives home the point about the low self-esteem we victims have.

Being brought up in the Southwest, I grew up with classmates who spoke Spanish much of the time. So I picked up bits and pieces of the language, usually the slang words and curse words first. I never could speak Spanish, but I could understand some of it.

When I woke awhile ago, I remembered a conversation with a guy I considered a friend—a buddy—in high school. We were talking during the lunch break, when he teasingly called me by some word in Spanish. I have no idea what word he used, but I remember being very defensive. I asked him, *"Does that mean anything like the word puta?* " (Nine-year-old *judy* was talking.)

The shock that registered on his face was sudden and complete. He backpedaled so fast to deny anything of the kind, that he stuttered. He reassured me that whatever word he had used was innocent and complimentary.

The word *puta* is Spanish for "whore." Because she couldn't say no, because she was so ashamed, *judy* thought of herself as a prostitute.

I weep for her lost sense of herself. She never knew she had any value in the world. If only someone could have loved her enough to show her who she really was.

Wednesday, August 16

My therapist, thank God, has been so careful of my boundaries when we've talked about sex. He knows the topic strikes fear into my heart, yet I will never be able to unravel this confusion until I learn to talk about it. It *is* okay to discuss sex with a counselor. Hard as it has been, it has helped.

Yesterday Jason asked me if I had ever felt depressed after orgasm. I cringed, wondering how he could know that. But it matches everything I wrote in the last couple of entries. Enjoying sex makes me bad because I fail to be in control. So I punish myself with depression.

I've always felt so alone in so many ways. Surely nobody else has ever been as confused as I have been. Nobody else has the sexual gaps I have. But my therapist knows how I feel because he's heard the same story so frequently. Therapists hear it all the time.

Victims of incest all feel as if they're the only ones. But we have so much in common. If only we could all find each other and know that it's safe to talk about the pain, the confusion, the loneliness. If only we could all know that it's not our fault. We aren't bad, after all.

Jason has used the word *confused* many times. Out of curiosity I looked it up in the dictionary to see if there was something about that word I was missing. What struck me was that *confused* is a past perfect *passive* verb. It takes an outside force acting on me to make me a confused person! Being confused is not being stupid or bad. Being confused is having had my thought processes scrambled, having some startling event disrupt my reasoning so that ordinary clarity is obscured. My natural, innocent state of reasoning as a child was clarity of thought. Someone else confused the way I viewed the world and relationships and sexuality, even my own value as a human being. My low self-esteem is a direct result of somebody mucking around in my brain.

And my greatest confusion has been on the topic of sexuality. Our sexual selves are the most private core of our being. That's why God intended monogamy as the perfect pattern. When there is damage done to our sexual self-concept, there is an intense degree of confusion in the deepest part of who we are.

No matter how we try to shrug off what happened and repress the memories so we can survive the days and years that follow, the damage to this most personal area of our individuality cannot be denied. Sexual abuse creates a festering wound that cannot heal in the atmosphere of shame and family secrecy that controls incest victims. Speaking the secret and opening that painful wound is the only way to release its poison.

Nobody likes to face surgery. But we've learned to trust doctors who tell us an operation is necessary for healing an advanced infection. I'm so glad I found a way to trust a therapist enough to finally open that ugly, gangrenous sore. I still hurt. But in the midst of the pain I know that this *is* the path to peace.

CHAPTER 4

Who Is God, Anyway?

Shifting my focus to exploring God's true nature was a relief from agonizing over abuse. I wondered if I was using this new topic as a tangent to avoid what I was <u>supposed</u> to be working on.

But it was only through understanding how completely God accepts me that I was able to trust Him enough to receive comfort and healing from Him. There is no <u>right</u> way to do therapy. This was the way I had to follow.

Friday, August 18, 11:30 P.M.

A few weeks back, Jason loaned me a tape called "Healing of Memories" by David Seamands. It's taken from the book by the same name, which I had read before. He asked me yesterday how I felt about the concept of memory healing.

I feel sort of strange about it. Psychologists call it regression or guided imagery. This is not the sort of interaction you might have with a friend over coffee. It's just not in the realm of my experience. It scares me.

Memory healing, as I understand it, is a prayer session where God's presence and active healing are invited while the counselor and the client talk specifically about a painful memory. I suppose it would be Jason talking with my inner child, a little like I have talked with her. Except that we would be back at the scene, almost as if it were happening again. And God would be there, too.

Seamands backs up memory healing with sound biblical support and tells stories of people who have been freed from traumatic memories much like mine. I want more than anything to be set free of this phantom that's been haunting me. I guess my difficulty in accepting memory healing is that I never saw God be actively engaged in anybody's life. It sounds a lot like asking for miracles, and I don't think I believe in miracles.

When I told Jason how I felt, he replied, "Maybe it's not a miracle we're asking for. Can't we ask God to be alive, to be involved in our lives? Hasn't He promised us that?"

"In theory, I suppose I can agree with that," I answered slowly. "But in practice, I'm afraid of it. Because, if I'm willing to ask him for that kind of action, I have to let Him be in charge. I have to submit to Him. And submission to God feels like submission to rape."

I continue to be surprised by words that pop out of my mouth, unbidden. I guess that means I'm not ready. I'm still afraid of God, and I'm afraid to go *back there* again and face the memories.

Thursday, August 24

I retained some interesting facts from the child development class I took a couple of years ago. One of them applies to the topic of spiritual abuse, which has shown up in several books I've read lately, especially in Seamands' books.

Children learn from the concrete to the abstract. They learn to count apples with Cookie Monster before they can manipulate abstract number concepts in their heads. Makes sense. A newborn infant learns first that Mommy feeds her and changes her and keeps her warm before she can understand that Mommy loves her. Concrete to abstract. But what if those basic needs aren't met consistently throughout childhood? Parents are like God to a little kid. They're concrete, palpable forms of a higher power, the only higher power she's ever known.

If that child learns that her physical and emotional needs are met only sporadically, then however much she may deny it on the surface, she knows in her guts that nobody cares about her. And she will translate that concrete knowledge into a belief about a higher abstract—that the universe is not a safe, loving place. When she knows the world to be cold and hard and shaming, how can she see God, the inventor of the whole system, as anything but judgmental and abusive? Maybe she'll try to please Him, just as she tries so hard to please her parents. She might even become a Christian and work, work, work to prove herself acceptable. But she won't ever feel good enough.

Like me. I see now how my inner child's real expectations of God don't match the theology I can recite so smoothly. I would never have admitted to not trusting God. I've always seen myself as an honest person, but I am amazed at the real content just beneath the surface. It looks like I learned to lie to myself to feel safer.

Tuesday, August 29, 2:30 A.M.

Awake again. I sure don't get as much sleep as I used to. How am I going to manage my college classes if I don't get more sleep? But here I am, so I may as well write.

I was remembering a class discussion back in my high school Bible study at church. I was always the first with my hand up to answer a question. Just like in school, my "performance" was my play for attention and acceptance. But it also set me up to be vulnerable.

In this instance the topic was "Why We Believe Dancing Is Wrong," which was a concept that never made sense to me. The argument was based on the contention that the movements in social dancing would tempt us to lustful thoughts. I could argue eloquently against such a position, but when it came down to obeying the edict against dancing, I submitted without a peep. It was just one more way I was different from everybody else.

I raised my hand and entered the fray, saying, "The fact that guys are going to have lustful thoughts watching girls dance isn't necessarily the fault of the dancing! Some guys are going to have lustful thoughts no matter what's going on. They'll be lusting looking at a girl just . . . just . . . sitting in a tree!"

As soon as the words were out of my mouth, I felt alarms going off in my head. I was embarrassed and ashamed. What kind of stupid example was that—sitting in a tree! I thought everyone else must be thinking how stupid I was, too. But I never connected why I "accidentally" chose those words.

Until now. I was the girl sitting in the tree, reading a book in full view of the neighborhood, because there wasn't any-place else that was safe. But somehow I must have done something to provoke lustful thoughts, because Gary still lusted after me. *It must be my fault because boys can't help lusting.*

What a heavy burden *judy* has carried all these years—believing herself responsible and guilty for any evil thought anyone else had about her. If she *had* danced, she would have felt responsible for other people's lust even more, because she *herself* was bait dangled deliberately, and she could have avoided it. Boys couldn't help it. *Lies!*

Wednesday, August 30, 11:45 P.M.

In my therapy session today, I told Jason about that class discussion. He pointed out an angle on that situation that hadn't occurred to me.

"Isn't it interesting," he said, "that your family chose a church with such a strict stance on dancing while at the same time they were, in effect, condoning Gary's molesting you by being in denial about the kind of person he was? Kind of like, 'It's okay that guys mess with little girls when nobody's looking—and we *sure* aren't going to *look*—but you'd better not move your body to music, because that's *really bad!*' What were they telling you about who God is while they were living out of two such conflicting attitudes?"

I didn't have an instant answer. But Jason did set the wheels in motion. That's the kind of assignment he usually gives me to work on after I leave his office. Just a simple, open-ended question that starts me off down a new corridor in my mind.

The rigid attitude about the *badness* of dancing (and smoking, drinking, and illicit sex, among other things) told me that God runs a very tight ship. He doesn't tolerate any of this self-indulgent frivolity designed for human enjoyment. He's got his eye on us, like Santa Claus: "He's makin' a list and checkin' it twice. Gonna find out who's naughty and nice . . ."

Combined with the fact that they ignored what Gary was doing, it told me that God is especially watching out to make sure *girls* aren't being bad. Gary (and Richard, too) was excused from having a raging temper. Gary (and all males) couldn't help their sexual impulses, so girls had to be in control. And if girls danced, they were deliberately waving temptation under the noses of the boys. So if they got raped, it was their own fault.

Of course none of this was ever spoken out loud. They'd all have denied it if I'd ever been able to put words around these shadowy perspectives that hung in the air. But they were lies nonetheless, even without the words.

I'm reminded of a quotation by Robert Louis Stevenson: "The cruelest lies are often told in silence." (I wonder what *his* family was like. Anything like mine?)

This is spiritual abuse! My picture of who God is couldn't be any more twisted. But I don't want to live by what *they* taught me about God. As long as I continue to relate to God (or refuse to relate to God) as the punishing being *they* taught me He was, then I am still at the mercy of their abuse.

So many of us raised in dysfunctional families have separated from our parents, grieved our losses, and worked for years to be healthy, yet call ourselves atheists because we won't submit to that concept of God we experienced back home. Don't we see how by holding God at a distance, we are still in submission to the lies our parents told us about Him? We are still living out of fear of that abusive higher power. And that abusive higher power turns out to be our parents . . . not God, after all!

Someone else once said, "Even liars sometimes tell the truth." We've been reacting to our parents' acknowledgment that God exists at all, whatever His nature! They were telling the truth when they said "God *is*", they just never had a clue to what He was really like.

Opening ourselves to the possibility of a loving heavenly Father makes us feel vulnerable, so we hang on to the illusion of control in rejecting God. If I reject Him first, He won't have the chance to rape me and reject me. Ugly picture.

I guess it's time to find out for myself who He really is, apart from the input of my family.

Saturday, September 2

I've begun my search for the *real* God in the Psalms, the book in the Bible I guess I'm most familiar with. It feels safe. The more I read, though, the more I am struck by the fact that I have always seen the Bible as dead words on a page. It feels so different now!

How could I have missed all my life that "God-breathed" inspiration was not *just* aimed at the humans who wrote down his message in the Bible! The words on these pages are God's voice whispered in my ear to teach me of His purpose and compassion for *me*—a single, insignificant individual living in the twentieth century!

David the shepherd wrote most of the Psalms. They were the songs of his soul, in pain and in joy. He was a terrible rascal, though—a confirmed sinner, yet at the same time, a man after God's own heart. Does this mean God really loves sinners?

For God to use a human being as contemptible as David was—an adulterer, a murderer, a liar—to hold him up as an example to His people, is astounding. Doesn't that mean there's hope that God could love *me*, too, however bad my inner child thinks she is?

Come to think of it, nearly every person portrayed in the Bible has made some whoppers of mistakes. God didn't try to cover over their flaws and sell us an "edited" version of their lives. Why not? Maybe it's because He *wanted* us to see them as imperfect humans.

Simon Peter kept bungling his attempts to serve Jesus. (Was something inside him sabotaging that service?) It was to Peter that Christ said, "Get thee behind me, Satan!" (Matt. 16:23 KJV). How that must have hurt! Especially after Peter denied Christ three times. He tried so hard, but his faith was weak. Yet it was Peter's faith that was the example Jesus used as the foundation of his kingdom: "Upon this rock I will build my church"! (16:18 KJV). Wow! Peter was privileged to be an intimate of Jesus and a leader in the infant church.

Abraham and Solomon, Jonah, the apostle Paul—God accepted each one of them, knowing their strengths and their weaknesses. He had created them, had known them in the womb, had designed a plan for each of their lives, all the while knowing the traps of sin they would fall into. In spite of their faults, God loved them.

I kept searching: "The Lord is compassionate and gracious, slow to anger, abounding in love. He will not always accuse, nor will He harbor His anger forever; He does not treat us as our sins deserve or repay us according to our iniquities.

For as high as the heavens are above the earth, so great is His love for those who fear Him; as far as the east is from the west, so far has He removed our transgressions from us. As a father has compassion on His children, so the Lord has compassion on those who fear Him; for He knows how we are formed, He remembers that we are dust" (Ps. 103:8–14, NIV).

He remembers that I am dust! He knows how flawed and fallible I am, and He forgives me, only because I have turned toward Him and received His mercy.

I wanted to know more: "How we praise God, the Father of our Lord Jesus Christ, who has blessed us with every blessing in heaven because we belong to Christ. Long ago, even before He made the world, God chose us to be his very own, through what Christ would do for us; He decided then to make us holy in His eyes, without a single fault—we who stand before Him covered with His love. His unchanging plan has always been to adopt us into His own family by sending Jesus Christ to die for us. And He did this because He wanted to!" (Eph. 1:3–5, TLB).

If I am a Christian, I am an adopted child. I was chosen before the Creation, even though God knew all along the shame that would haunt me for so much of my life. God saw the sins committed against me and *by* me even then, and He forgave them. He designed a plan to use that evil for my eventual good.

This is such a different picture of God! One I can come to trust. Maybe I can believe He *is* willing to be active in my healing after all.

Yet, as comforting as this is to me, I am still living night and day with such heaviness of spirit! This burden of incest is the first thing I think of in the morning and the last at night. I am beginning to see God differently, but I still hurt constantly!

Sunday, September 3, 1:30 A.M.

I finally recognized the missing piece in the last journal entry I made—*women*. Part of my old view of God seems to be that God has different standards for men and women. Exploring the profiles of David and Peter is illuminating, but it doesn't address that gap.

So what does God think about women? Does He accept them in the same way, even though men are more visible in the Bible?

I heard a sermon once on the genealogy of Jesus as found in Matthew. It comes to mind now as a pretty strong statement on God's attitude about women. The Jews were really big on genealogy. Tradition dictated that they trace their lineage through the males in the line. They documented the "purity" of their chromosomes by going back all the way to Abraham.

But Jesus' genealogy doesn't look so pure. Every single person mentioned in Jesus' genealogy was a sinner, whether we know their stories or not. Some of the stories we *do* know are pretty shameful. Also, five women were included in the list, and women, in that day, were never included!

Every one of those women had something in her history that society would have deemed sin, yet Jesus wasn't ashamed to have them proclaimed as His family.

Tamar was on the list. She seduced her father-in-law (Gen. 38:1–10). Perez was one of the of twins born to her as a result of that *incestuous* union with her husband's father! And Perez (a bastard) is directly in the genetic line as an ancestor of the Messiah. Jesus wasn't ashamed of Tamar?

Rahab was the mother of Boaz, but she was also the prostitute who hid the two spies Joshua had sent to check out the city of Jericho (Josh. 2). Current statistics claim that somewhere between sixty and ninety percent of prostitutes have been sexually abused, not including the ones who won't admit it or don't remember it. If the background for becoming a prostitute today is that one's self-worth and ideas about sex have been confused by sexual abuse, it makes sense that Rahab may have had the same reason. Incest again? Maybe. We'd certainly call her a sinner even if that theory doesn't hold. But Jesus wasn't ashamed of Rahab!

Then there's Ruth, who was a Gentile. No Jew in his right mind would have considered marrying a Gentile back then. (Of course, Boaz, who married her, was the son of a prostitute, so who was he to point fingers?) But Ruth must have been deemed worthy, because a book of the Bible was named for her, and we hold her up as an example of faithfulness.

I seem to remember reading somewhere, though, that perhaps Ruth's act of lying down at Boaz' feet was a polite, culturally accepted way of saying she would have sex with him. It was certainly an offer of herself. (Naomi had advised Ruth to do that, saying, "He will tell you what to do." The implication is that Ruth was willing to follow his bidding, even if it meant having sex with somebody she'd seen only once.) But here she is in the genealogy. Hmmm.

Bathsheba—the most famous adulteress in the Old Testament—was the mother of Solomon, David's son, after David committed adultery with her and had her first husband killed. Am I out on a limb here, or do I see a trend of sexual sin for all these women? But Bathsheba is on the genealogy list, too.

And then there's Mary, the mother of Jesus. We get all swept up in the miracle of the virgin birth, but Mary's friends and family probably had a different perspective on things. Jesus was not universally acknowledged to be the actual Son of God by the Holy Spirit. Mary must have been the subject of gossip, and the general belief of the day had to be that her story about an angel was "hogwash"! But God didn't seem to mind what conclusions people came to.

He accepted all those women and acknowledged their place in the lineage of Christ. He even highlighted their roles, when their names could have been left out entirely. I think I see an attitude of forgiveness, as if he sees beyond our sins and even *expects* us to be sinners!

In the New Testament, every encounter Jesus had with a woman showed only compassion and healing. The adulteress could legally have been stoned, but got off with a gentle "Go, and sin no more." The woman at the well had five husbands. (Multiple sexual relationships are one of the symptoms of sexual abuse!) Jesus knew her whole history (like He knows mine?), yet offered her living water. The sinful woman who anointed His feet was forgiven her sins. He seemed to hang out with a lot of people with bad reputations, women included.

How can I see all these examples of Jesus' forgiveness of women and not believe He has compassion on me? Maybe He'd want me to forgive myself, to have compassion on that child inside me who believes she's *bad*, to love her, instead.

Tuesday, September 5, 10:30 P.M.

God does work in mysterious ways. I hardly slept at all the last two nights, yet nothing came to mind to work on, and I resisted writing. I didn't understand it, and I've been worn out and cranky.

Today, in a mental fog of exhaustion, I went to my first day of college classes for the fall semester. I registered for ten hours, making sure my classes were easier than last spring, when my life was falling apart just before I started counseling. But sitting through the first classes, as tired as I was, I felt so overwhelmed it was if I were going to suffocate. I couldn't get out of there fast enough. Even the ceramics class seemed like an impossible task. What made me think I could do this?

After thinking about it all day and praying about it, I still didn't get the message until I sat down with my husband after dinner and heard myself say, "I don't think God means me to be in school this semester!"

David just smiled. "That's a good thought."

Well, David, (and Jason, too), has trusted me to make whatever decision was right for me. Of course, they both know me well enough to know that I'm not going to be easily dissuaded once I'm set on a direction. Stubborn? Yes.

The Lord's priority for me right now is therapy. I thought I could breeze back into school and slow the pace of therapy—back to once a week—and fit it all in with my part-time job, my roles as a wife and mother, and my still-compulsive reading.

But God isn't backing down on therapy, and if it takes keeping me awake a few nights to remind me it's not as simple as it used to be, then He'll do that to make sure I get the picture. He's actually paying attention to the petty details of my life!

I think He's teaching me submission, too. But it feels a whole lot different from my old idea of submission. I can submit and drop this semester of classes because I can see He's in charge anyway, and He's going to work it all out for my good.

It looks as if God is taking action in my life to show me He *is* an active God. I'm more comfortable with the idea of being with Him than I was. Prayer feels good now, and it never did before. I think He's guiding me, and teaching me to trust Him.

Sunday, September 17, 7:00 P.M.

Jason recommended I read *Knowing God*, a book by J.I. Packer, since I was already working on seeing God as He really is. At first, I flew through it, though it's not light reading. It was eye-opening stuff! I sped through chapters on God's nature: God unchanging, God's majesty, God's wisdom, God's truth, God's love, God's grace . . . until I came to chapters on God the judge, God's wrath, God's severity. And I stalled out.

I explained what was happening to Jason on Thursday. As soon as the words were out of my mouth, I knew why I had lurched to a stop. This was familiar and frightening terrain, because these were the characteristics I had always seen in God. I *feared* God's wrath, His severity and judgment because I was *bad*. The trouble was that I had been seeing only a small part of God. Yes, God does have anger for sin. But the change comes when we call out for help.

I *did* call out for help when I was little and alone. But the abuse didn't stop, so I thought God wasn't listening. Is it possible He really did hear me and responded in a way I didn't recognize?

I've always thought of myself as a strong person . . . externally, at least. In control. Was that strength an endowment at conception, along with brown hair and hazel eyes? Maybe it was, instead, a gift of grace in response to my prayer for help.

Was my love for reading His gift in answer to my prayer? It kept me sane by creating a way to escape the shame and pretend to be somebody else. Did He give me my capacity for codependency? Pretty raggedy coping skills for an adult, but they were my means of avoiding greater pain as a child. Did He give me my ability to repress those awful memories? Living with the conscious awareness of what happened every day would probably have driven me to suicide. He kept me from that somehow. Maybe He *was* active in my life all along, but I didn't know where to look to find Him.

Now I am beginning to see that my life could have been worse. I had blessings I never recognized. As much as I feared my stepfather, could he really have been my friend? His fury directed at Gary might have been because he could see what my brother really was. It was Richard who wanted to send Gary away to military school, but Mom wouldn't hear of it.

Was Richard trying to keep Gary away from me? I never understood.

There have been other people along the way who have given me little bits of themselves and comforted me to the degree that I could receive it. And I've been led to my therapist so I can be healed. I guess I've had to hit bottom to be able to look up. Yes, God is good. I'll finish reading *Knowing God*.

Tuesday, September 19, 2:30 A.M.

My waking in the middle of the night still isn't a welcome ritual, but it's certainly a familiar one. I used to be irritated that I wasn't getting my quota of sleep. But lately I see my insomnia as quiet time with the Lord. "Be still and know that I am God." Well, maybe 2:00 A.M. is the only time I'm still enough that He can get my attention!

I feel like Samuel in the Bible, roused from sleep by the call of the Lord. While I haven't heard a voice in the way Samuel did, I am frequently surprised by an unexpected insight into an issue that's been bothering me when I write in the middle of the night. So I'm more willing to wake up and hear the message.

Psalm 23 has been running through my mind lately, but lying in bed just now, I suddenly saw an amazingly obvious contrast that had previously escaped me.

The Lord is my Shepherd. Jehovah—self-existent, eternal God, the sovereign Lord, author and Creator of the universe, holy and just King over all—is Judy's (and *judy's*) Shepherd. Just the way He was for David and Moses and the apostles and for every other single soul He created . . . even incest victims.

A shepherd doesn't sit on a golden throne and direct regal proceedings with an airy wave of his jewel-laden hand. A shepherd sleeps in the field with a rock for a pillow.

He hangs out with the stupidest of animals—sheep. Sheep are filthy, foul-smelling beasts, always walking into the most obvious of traps. They trot blithely into the den of a lion and bleat in panic for rescue. Sheep walk over the edges of cliffs or let their curiosity lead them into impossibly precarious positions from which they have no hope of escape. The shepherd has to bail them out over and over again.

Yet the shepherd doesn't curse the sheep for their stupidity. He knows they can't help it. He leaves the ninety-nine and chases after the lost one before that solitary lamb may even be aware of its predicament. The shepherd always keeps a head count and knows when they're in trouble, before they even call for help.

The shepherd knows He can't drive sheep the way he could drive cattle. He has to gain the trust of the sheep and then lead them, by showing them the way and by looking out for the ones who aren't following.

The Lord has arranged the universe so that He is constantly soiling His hands by reaching out to us poor dumb sheep, who don't even know enough to be grateful. Sheep think they're in control of their own destinies. So do we. But the Lord is my Shepherd.

judy needs a picture like that. A child needs to know that, no matter what awful things she's done or someone else has done to her, she is Jesus' little lamb, cradled in His arms. Safe.

I think He's giving me a second wind. I think He'll give me strength to take my eyes off the pain and to focus instead on Him and the hope He gives me in His purpose for the rest of my life. Courage is not the absence of fear, but the strength to go on through fear and not let it stop you. I guess I'm finally at a place that I can trust God to fulfill His promise to me—that He will give me the strength and courage to bear whatever comes.

Armed with that thought, I can acknowledge the fear and trembling, yet face the memories that have to be faced. Is this a turning point?

CHAPTER 5

Going Back

<u>Why does it have to be sex?</u> *judy* kept wanting
to know. To talk about those shameful things
went against every instinct for self-preservation.
But <u>not</u> talking about it hadn't healed the pain.
I couldn't see any hope but to trust Jason.

Eventually I came to recognize that, when
there was strong resistance to verbalizing an
issue, it probably meant a special need to get
beyond the resistance and talk about it. That defense was to protect a deep wound needing the
healing that only confession would bring.

Friday, September 22, 2:30 A.M.

After staring at this page for a very long time, I force myself to begin at last, to quiet the churning in my guts. A therapist really knows how to open a can of worms!

"We may need to find one or two more memories with Gary," Jason said at the end of my session yesterday.

I had cautiously acknowledged the need to talk specifically about what happened. And he had responded, "I don't know any other way for it to be healed." As much as I hate the idea of going *back there*, I know he's right. I have to go through it to get past it. But willingly seeking more memories?

"We don't have to dredge up every buried instance, but enough to access the feelings associated with the abuse. Just remember," he emphasized, "you have already survived it. And you aren't alone this time."

Well, suddenly there is another memory—one that gags me to think about. But stuffing it back into the box will not further the healing process, I guess, so here goes.

Bringing up this incident makes my whole body stiffen and draw back reflexively, which I'm sure matches the original response. I'm feeling *fear*. Putting the words on paper is as difficult as telling Jason in a session. But I trust my counselor, or I would never have come to this point. Deep breath.

In the third grade (when I was nine, I guess), some kid in my neighborhood asked me if I knew where babies came from. *No! Tell me!* My curiosity turned to revulsion at the explanation he gave. Back at home, I asked for confirmation of the story from Gary and Carla. And Gary took my innocent question as the occasion to offer more information. This must have been the first time! He took me aside and told me to come to his room after lights out.

Going to Gary's room opens up the topic of my responsibility again, because his room is where it happened. I have this enormous feeling of dread just writing down those words, but it will feel worse if I don't. So I force my hand to write.

Gary assumed the role of "sex instructor." He took off my nightgown and panties, and, touching me, told me the words for parts of my anatomy. Nasty words, for dirty parts of me. I'm sure I didn't speak at all; I was having a hard enough time breathing!

He stroked my flat chest, telling me how my—oh, the word he used! That word, such a flagrantly derogatory, mocking term for a part of me—a humiliation word—has always made me irrationally furious. How dare he make fun of my body? I couldn't help how I was made!

Then he had his clothes off, too, and he showed me his "thing." He told me to touch it. I did, in horrified fascination. I am screaming on the inside just writing this, and I can't finish. . . .

All that is holding me together is Philippians 1:6. I have a promise that God will be faithful to finish this work He began in me. I won't be stuck, hanging off this cliff forever.

September 24, 3:00 A.M.

judy is so afraid. I try to be quiet when I'm up during the night, so I won't wake David or my daughters. But I can hear *her* screaming silently, deep inside me. Somehow those screams have to be released, or both of us will go crazy. Writing them, in a way, is giving voice to her screams.

Do you think I'm __bad__?

No, child. No. Remember? Jason said a long time ago, that it is *never* the responsibility of the child when there is sexual abuse. Never. Even if a child behaves seductively, she has learned it through a previous victimization. You only wanted to be loved.

But I went to his room! I could have told him no.

The word no didn't exist for you, did it? Without ever having been given a choice about anything in your life, did you feel as though you had a choice about going to his room?

He made me. I was scared of him. It was like I was a zombie, and he had some kind of remote control over my brain. I tried not to, but part of me wanted to go, because it felt good. He made me bad.

No, not bad. Only helpless and vulnerable and confused. Nobody was there to help you understand. It's natural to want to feel good, and those feelings you got were the only good ones you knew about. No matter how many times it happened, no matter how or where it happened, it was never you who was in control. It was never you who was being bad, because you never had a choice.

Jason believes in you. He'll be with us going *back there*. He won't shame you for what happened. I trust him, and I trust God now, and it's going to be safe. Nobody's going to hurt you anymore.

Now rest. You don't have to be the grown-up. You don't have to be in charge. I'll take care of you. Rest.

Wednesday, September 27, 10:00 P.M.

My inner child wants so much to believe what I tell her. But she's never felt safe before, and she still doesn't feel safe, when sex seems to be the topic in every therapy session and talking about the specifics looms just ahead. I hear her voice at odd times—driving down the street or cooking dinner (not that I do *that* very often)—*Why does it have to be sex?* How often have I heard that question in my head? And *Why do we have to talk about it?*

Well, I can't help that the topic is sex. The topic for my life has been sex since the first time I was molested. She doesn't want to talk about it. Saying the words is shameful. But it's exactly because the words are shameful that they have to be said.

Specifics validate our experience. Family secrecy never allowed us to have words to frame what happened to us. I could live all my life in denial, saying that my family was only weird, until I was able to verbalize specifically what happened. Only then could I acknowledge the truth.

If I ask a medical doctor to heal a wound in my physical body, he will insist that I remove the four layers of clothing covering it up. He has to examine the hurt first. For a therapist to help me heal a spiritual and emotional wound, he will ask me to remove the rationalizations and defense mechanisms disguising it. We have to examine the hurt. We have to assess the extent of the damage, so the cure will be complete.

Jesus said the truth will set us free, but when it's hidden in generalities, we are still insulated from it, not letting ourselves *feel* the pain we suffered. We may still believe the lie that it wasn't so bad.

1 John 1:8 says, "If we say that we have no sin, we deceive ourselves, and the truth is not in us" (NKJV). Well, denial of our own sins and denial of the sins others have committed against us are two sides of the same coin. Minimization, deceiving ourselves about *all* sin is our unwillingness to face reality, and the truth is not in us. So how can we be set free?

God knows us better than anybody. He sees our specific needs for help and healing. Still, He tells us to "ask," "seek," and "knock." Why? Because He knows *we* don't see our needs until we are able to verbalize them specifically to *Him*. And

71

we aren't able to receive His healing if we can't understand our own need.

Saying the words about what happened back then draws us out of denial and allows us to admit our need. And it breaks the chains that secrecy creates. That's how we're kept in bondage to sin—by pretending it doesn't exist. They don't call Satan the Prince of Darkness for nothing. Nothing pleases him more than the darkness of the secrecy that surrounds incest. Because when we expose it to the light of Christ, we aren't bound by it anymore.

Of course, this is all great on paper, and I can say all the right words intellectually, but I've seen how much my inner child is in control. She's still struggling. But she knows the words have to be spoken.

Thursday, September 28, 4:00 P.M.

How can I express the relief I am feeling? I walked into my therapy appointment today, filled with apprehension. I left with a song in my heart! And with hope.

Jason touched my shoulder as I came in, and I savored the contact. Is this what a father's touch would have felt like? Safe like this? He asked me how I was feeling, and I gave him an honest answer. "Afraid." He nodded. That didn't surprise him.

We talked for a few minutes about how I'd learned to trust him and to trust God. He prayed with me, asking for God's presence, protection, and guidance. Then he said, "Is your inner child with you today?"

I gave him a shaky smile. "She's always with me." I guess that was her, wanting Jason's touch.

He asked if I'd be more comfortable with my eyes open or closed. If my eyes were closed, I wouldn't have to worry about eye contact. I shut them.

He asked me to count slowly backward, from ten to one. I did, wishing this were over, instead of just beginning. "Do you think your inner child would be willing to talk to me about what happened with Gary?"

Twisting a tissue in my lap, I took a breath, and nodded.

"*judy*?" Jason asked quietly.

Strangely, I had the sensation of gliding helplessly backward as if on tracks that pulled me smoothly away from Jason, to observe from a detached position. But I was still in the chair.

"*Yes?*" It was a quavery whisper, and *her* voice was all I could muster. As quickly as that! Where was my adult self control?

"How old are you, *judy*?"

I searched for a reasonable answer, but *her* voice responded again, "*Nine.*"

"Can you tell me what happened when you went to Gary's room?" Jason spoke very slowly. Gently. He knew he was talking to a terrorized child.

"*He . . . touched me.*" Her voice was barely audible. My heart pounded.

"Were you wearing your nightgown?"

Pause. "*No,*" I gulped for breath. "*. . . he . . . took it off.*" Already I was fighting back tears.

"And he touched your breasts?"

She was ashamed to answer such a question. "*Yes.*"

"Did he put his finger into your vagina?"

"*Yes.*" Just the whispered monosyllable was painful to release. It was hard to breathe.

"And then . . . did he tell you to do something?"

"*He . . . made me touch his penis. . . . But I didn't want to!*"

"No. You didn't want to. Did . . . he make a mess on your hand?"

I felt myself jerk back reflexively in my chair. *"I ... guess ... he did."* Wanting to scream, it came out more like a low moan.

I sensed Jason shifting in his chair a little. "You've been locked in that room with Gary for a very long time. Would you like to get out of that room, *judy*?"

"Yes!" Oh, how I wanted out!

"Jesus is there with you, in that room, *judy*. If you turn your head just a little, you can see Him. Do you see Him?"

"Yes!" And I did! There He stood, by the door.

"Jesus has been watching everything that happened. Can you see how angry He is that Gary hurt you?"

I nodded, surprised at the fierce intensity in Jesus' eyes.

"Just the look on Jesus' face is enough to stop Gary. Gary sees Him, too, and he's afraid, because he can see how much Jesus hates the sin that hurts innocent children. Can you see Jesus putting His hand on Gary's arm?"

I watched Jesus walk across the room to lay His big rough hand on Gary's arm.

"Yes." Gary seemed to freeze in place.

"And Gary is taking his hands off you. He's not touching you anymore. You can move away from Him now. You can put your clothes back on. When you're dressed again, lift one finger to let me know."

I watched myself move away, shaking, and slowly pull on my nightgown and underwear. When I was covered, I found the strength to raise one finger in my lap.

"Would you like Jesus to come close to you?"

I answered with a barely perceptible nod. I couldn't speak.

"Can you ask Jesus to move near you?"

I hesitated. To speak to Him, after what He had just *seen*? How could I? The shame welled up in my throat and choked back my words. Finally I pushed aside my fear and forced myself to see Jesus' face. The compassion in his eyes gave me the courage to whisper, *"Will you be with me, Jesus?"*

Jesus reached out to me and enclosed my small, trembling hand in the strength of His grip. And then I felt His powerful arms surrounding me, drawing me close to His heart. His love filled me with warmth. I was safe, with Him.

"Jesus won't let Gary hurt you anymore, *judy*. He's going to protect you. But before He takes you out, He's turning to look at Gary again. As much as He hates the sin in what your brother did, how does Jesus feel about Gary himself?"

Now that I was safe by his side, I saw the fury Jesus had directed at Gary's actions soften into sorrow. *"He's . . . sad . . . for Gary,"* I said wonderingly.

"Yes. Jesus sees that Gary is hurting, too. Do you think Gary needs forgiveness for what he's just done?"

I focused on the panic in my brother's eyes and knew the depth of his shame. *"Yes."*

"judy, can you allow Jesus to forgive Gary now?"

But Gary had never invited God into his life! He'd never repented! Would Jesus offer him forgiveness anyway? Then I thought of the Lord's words from the cross: "Father, forgive them, for they know not what they do." He was speaking of Gary even then. Perhaps Gary's heart would never open enough to *receive* Jesus' forgiveness, but . . . could I allow Jesus to extend forgiveness to him?

Suddenly Gary seemed so small and weak. I'd never seen him that way before. All his power was gone. *"Yes,"* I answered at last.

"Jesus *has* forgiven him. What do you think Jesus would want *you* to say to Gary?"

"I . . . forgive you, Gary." Even with the difficulty in saying the words, I knew this forgiveness would be real. Gary didn't matter anymore.

"Jesus loves Gary enough to forgive him for hurting you. Does Jesus love you, *judy*?"

I nodded. *Yes, Jesus loves me. The Bible tells me so.*

"Jesus has seen you struggling under that heavy burden of the hatred you've carried for so long, *judy*. You've hated Gary, and you've hated yourself, haven't you?"

I nodded miserably, choking back a sob that threatened to escape.

"Jesus never wanted you to torment yourself the way you have. He's been hurt to see His child—you—do such injury to yourself. You've condemned yourself without mercy all these years, while God hasn't judged you at all. Is your opinion of that vulnerable child more important than the way God sees you?"

I shook my head, feeling my heart breaking apart in my chest. Hating. Here was my *real* responsibility.

"Do you need His forgiveness, *judy*, for judging so harshly, for putting yourself above God's compassion?"

"*Oh!*" The word jumped out of its own volition. "*Yes.*"

"Why don't you ask Jesus for his forgiveness."

Ask! Had I ever been able to ask for anything and know it would be given to me without ridicule or rejection? But . . . Jesus is different. I looked up again into Jesus' face. The tenderness of His smile encouraged me to manage the words, "*Will you forgive me, Jesus?*"

"Has He forgiven you?" Jason asked after a slight pause.

"*Yes!*" Jesus' arms bore me up, out of that old shame. I felt such relief!

"Who else needs to forgive *judy*, for being in Gary's room that night?"

I wasn't quite sure what Jason meant. "*Me?*" I said at last.

"Well, have you ever forgiven yourself for what happened?"

I shook my head. "*No.*"

"Are you ready to forgive that frightened child for not knowing how to say no?"

I nodded.

"She needs to hear you say that."

Pause. "I forgive you." My adult self reluctantly came back long enough to choke out those difficult words.

"She has needed your acceptance for so long. She needs you to love her." Jason was quiet for a long moment. "Now. Are you ready to leave that room behind you?"

"*Yes!*" I breathed in relief.

"All right. Now Jesus is taking you by the hand and opening the bedroom door. Now you're out in the hallway. Do you turn left, or right, to get to the front door of the house?"

"*Left in the hall, then right through the living room,*" piped the nine-year-old voice.

"You're turning left in the hall, then right through the living room," Jason said. "Now Jesus is opening the front door and the two of you are outside, free of that house, and what happened inside that house, in Gary's room." He paused while I collected myself. "Is there a special place for you to go at home, somewhere you feel safe?"

I cast about in my mind for an answer. Was there safety anywhere? Except . . ."*I used to go out at night and lie in the grass to look at the stars. We lived at a high altitude, and the stars looked like a million diamonds on black velvet. Not like in the city.*"

"I don't think you ever told me that," said Jason quietly. "Would you like to share that with Jesus?"

I nodded silently. Tears were spilling down my cheeks.

"Then from the front door, with Jesus holding your hand, walk out to the grass and choose a place. Tell me when you're comfortable."

I watched myself settle beside Jesus on the grass, then raised a trembling right index finger.

"Is Jesus close to you?"

"He's lying on my right side. My head is on His shoulder, and He's holding my hand."

"Do you think Jesus has seen those stars before?"

I couldn't help grinning through my tears. *"He made them for me!"*

"He made them for you?"

"He knew me before He made the stars. He had me in mind. He knew they'd comfort me."

"Yes. He knew all that. He had a plan for you even then, a plan for you to be healed of the fear and pain of that night in Gary's room. Now . . . just lie there and rest and be at peace, with Jesus at your side. Know that He loves you. He doesn't think you were bad. He knows you were innocent. He wants to protect you. Know that He will always be with you."

"If you should find yourself back in that room with Gary, any time at all, all you have to do is ask Jesus to take you out, and you can see Him leading you out to the stars. That night with Gary can't have any more power over you, because Jesus has freed you from that bondage. Now just relax. And when you're ready to come back into the office with me, you can open your eyes."

As I opened my eyes, Jason smiled at me and wiped his own eyes as I cried tears of relief. And tears of joy at feeling Jesus' presence, His forgiveness.

If I hadn't experienced it, I don't know if I could have believed it. That weight on my chest isn't so heavy. I'm sure there's more work to do, but I *can* believe in miracles, because that rancid, festering wound doesn't hurt so much now. Thank God.

Tuesday, October 3, 8:00 P.M.

The change I feel is amazing. It's not that I don't hurt anymore, but I have joy in the midst of the hurting. A window has been opened above me so I can see the stars, and fresh air has rushed into the oppressive closeness of that child's soul. I can breathe!

judy has spent all her life in fear and in anger at the unfairness of it all. *Why me? Why did I have to live through this?* She's taken it out on my children and on my husband, because he's a man.

The world isn't fair. A child should never have to go through that horror, with no one to help her understand it. But I can see that God's healing transcends our concept of time. Even now He can go back to that night and comfort her, when she needed comforting so badly.

I have felt at last the touch of my heavenly Father's hand—the only father that matters. Reaching up in my weak, faltering faith, He has stretched out his hand to meet mine. Enclosed my aching heart in his love. Yeah, God still does make housecalls.

Friday, October 6, 1:30 A.M.

No, I'm not done yet. Jason asked me yesterday, "Do you feel a weight?"

"You mean a weight lifted? Or here . . . on my chest?" My fist thumped against my chest as if pulled there by a powerful magnet.

As always, he left it to my own interpretation. Jason doesn't feed me too many lines. He lets me draw my own conclusions. "You tell me," he said.

"Well, I've felt like I have a thirty-pound anvil sitting on my chest."

"That may be the sensation of weight that is called a 'body memory.' Very commonly victims of childhood sexual abuse describe that same feeling of weight. Like the mass of a larger body on top of their smaller body, making it difficult to breathe."

Great. So that sensation—a classic symptom of incest—is another confirmation of intercourse. But what he said next set off more alarms.

"There's another response you've shown that may be a body memory also . . ." He paused.

Well? Well? Don't keep me in suspense!

"No, I think I'll hold that for another time."

I didn't get it at the time, but now, at 2:00 A.M., I know what he meant. And this writing is another scream in the night—to let out what keeps circulating through my mind.

The other body memory is difficulty breathing and my throat hurting all the time, like a chunk of granite is lodged there. I've tried to ignore it. I've written it off to stress. It's also one of the seven warning signs of cancer, and I *knew* I didn't want it to be that. Naaah. My allergies are just draining into my throat. Or I'm catching a cold.

No. The truth is that my aching throat is the message that there was oral sex. To a frightened little girl, was that somehow a worse violation than vaginal penetration? Maybe it was because I'd been told not to put dirty things in my mouth. And if sex is bad, what could be dirtier than a penis?

Oh, no! I finally understand the hidden meaning in my old recurring dream about driving up the side of the mountain. The mountain moved and groaned, and the angle became more and more steep. *Like an erect penis.* I remember my throat hurting when I wrote about it, close to the start of therapy. No wonder Jason wouldn't accept my interpretation that it was only about my perfectionism. I told him that dream before I ever acknowledged sexual abuse. But he had to have known, even then. That dream painted a graphic picture of oral sex. Just look at the way I wrote it! "I woke with an unborn scream *filling my throat*"!

Body memories are another way of reexperiencing the events that caused so much shame. *judy* has no more strength to hold it all down in my subconscious anymore. She's exhausted from living *back there* all these years, immersed in the lies that kept her chained to a bed. So she's letting me know the truth at last. Poor child.

Monday, October 9, 3:00 A.M.

Can't I have a break, God? Can't I rest awhile? No. So I'll write what just occurred to me, because avoidance doesn't help. Argument won't make it go away.

When David and I had been married about a year, we went to see the movie, *The Exorcist*. As soon as it came out, it made national headlines because it seemed to affect audiences more intensely than any previous horror movie.

Women, in amazing numbers, were fainting and throwing up and running out of theaters in panic. But I was strong and in control, and I could handle a scary flick . . . I thought.

I didn't throw up. I didn't flee the theater. But I was filled with the most intense fear in my memory. My heart raced wildly and I gripped David's hand so hard I nearly broke his fingers.

For six months afterward I acted weird. I had nightmares. I was hypersensitive to noises at night. I was afraid of my shadow! David vowed never to take me to another horror movie.

Suddenly I can see why I had that response. My behavior wasn't so weird, after all. As powerfully as guided imagery, but without the healing, I was drawn back into a painful scene in my past. I was reliving a flashback! I went *back there* without warning, without a counselor to help me face it. I was the victim again, all alone. Like the twelve-year-old girl in the movie, I was paralyzed on a bed, possessed by an evil male that made me *bad*, that made me want sex. I was helpless under his control.

Were the thousands of women who panicked over that movie victims of childhood incest, too? Here was a graphic picture that your mother cannot protect you, that evil dominates little girls and turns them into freaks. Of course we were afraid. We were unexpectedly confronted again with that same heart-stopping powerlessness that had shamed us so many times before.

I only wish I could have absorbed the happy ending. God won out at the end of the movie. Like God is winning in my life now. That evil spirit *is* being exorcised. I can smell freedom.

CHAPTER 6

Mama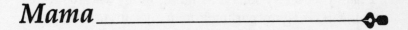

When I look back at what I've written, a little part of me still wants to protest, <u>But it wasn't that bad!</u> Old denial dies very hard. Especially when it comes to Mom.

My mother's love is what I wanted more than anything else in the world, and I still long for a connection with her that may never exist.

Friday, October 13, 5:00 P.M.

I had a hard day today. Standing in my bathroom this morning, holding my curling iron in my hair, my eyes wandered to a framed art print hanging on the wall. Suddenly I had that now-familiar clutch in my guts that comes with a terrible insight.

My glance rested on a print of an impressionistic painting of a mother and child, "The Cradle," by Berthe Morisot. The mother lovingly keeps watch over her sleeping infant. It's a picture that has given me peace. That's why I bought it. Seeing it now with new eyes, I know it's a lie. That's the mother I always wanted to have, the mother I told myself I had all along. But it isn't *my* mom.

I was instantly in tears as my throat closed around a painful lump. I laid the curling iron on the counter and walked slowly over to the wall.

Hanging immediately beside the first is a smaller frame holding a print of "After the Bath," by an artist named Peel. Two naked preschool-age girls are holding their hands out to warm themselves in front of a Victorian-style fireplace. I always loved that print. But now I wondered what lecherous eyes were watching them, out of the artist's line of sight. Two sisters in the age of innocence . . . before they get raped.

I want to shout a warning to those little girls, "Cover yourselves, run away before they hurt you!" But where? There isn't any safe place. There's nowhere to hide. There isn't any mother who will protect them.

I turned and saw the other prints I had collected over a period of several years. As well as I knew those pictures, it was as if I stood in a museum art gallery, studying each picture for the first time. Images of mother love. Childhood purity. Innocence, purity, and virginity that I was never allowed to have. Luxuries I never knew.

My favorite artists—Renoir, Mary Cassatt, Jessie Wilcox Smith—were all known for their portraits of mothers and children. And I was drawn to them because I wanted to fill that giant need in myself. I needed a mother.

So now I have a whole new tidal wave of grief for the loss of that illusion-mother I made myself believe in. The cardboard image I thought I had already sent over a cliff in a bus, has gone up in flames. My mother never loved me or protected me. That is truth.

Don't tell me this grieving is less than the loss of a mother through death! My dreams have died. I never had a mother.

Saturday, October 17, 1:45 A.M.

I woke up just now from a dream of some "ideal" mother reaching out to comfort me as a child. I stretched out my arms to her to be held, and the image evaporated. As always. The opposite of love isn't hate, is it? It's indifference.

My inner child needs to talk, I think. *judy,* are you awake? Tell me about Mom.

It hurts to think about Mama. She didn't care about me. She used to tell me the story of when Grandpa died and she took me back home with her for the funeral. Gary and Carla stayed with Jack's parents—our "real" grandparents. The trip was two long days on a Greyhound bus, and she was trying to wean me. From the breast to the bottle? From the bottle to a cup? I don't know.

She's told me how I screamed during the whole trip. The bus driver and the passengers were mad at her. The way she told me that story felt like it was my fault. I was a bad <u>baby, so everybody on the bus was upset with her.</u>

85

Couldn't she see that I needed her? Weaning me wasn't import-ant on a two-day bus trip when everything familiar to me was suddenly gone! But she was so wrapped up in her own pain that she had no idea how afraid I was. And in all the years, she never saw my needs any more clearly than that.

I hated her for rejecting me from the beginning. Did it have to do with the divorce? It wasn't my fault my father didn't want us! I couldn't help being born in the midst of the world war my parents fought between themselves.

I always thought she didn't love me because of who I was. But it was really something inside her, wasn't it? It wasn't my fault. I always tried so hard, but it didn't make any difference. It wasn't my fault.

No, it wasn't your fault. You were only a child. You couldn't change who she was.

Friday, October 20, 2:30 A.M.

I wonder if I even get three nights a week of uninterrupted sleep. I don't think so. Tonight the poet's awake. *judy* wrote:

> *Mama never gave me*
> *Birthday parties,*
> *Comforting arms,*
> *Soft hair shining from brushing*
> *And brushing. . . .*
> *Reassuring words spoken soft,*
> *Last kisses before peaceful sleep,*
> *Crisp ironed dresses,*
> *Pride in being me,*
> *A welcoming kitchen that invited friends,*
> *A special gladness to be female,*
> *Anything of herself,*
> *A way to understand the pain,*
> *Or childhood.*

Tuesday, October 24, 1:30 A.M.

I used to think therapy was what happened when you were sitting in a chair in the counselor's office. But that's just when the fuses are lit. Therapy is the firecrackers (and sometimes sticks of dynamite) that explode throughout the week between appointments. My counselor's leading questions blast open new excavations every time.

I could, of course, resist the follow-through, but then the shame would just circulate through my head for the rest of my life. Like the song from "It's a Small World" at Disneyland, you can't rid yourself of it for the remainder of your vacation. I'd rather write it out, to silence the tape of whatever awful recognition is exposed by the blasting.

Jason asked me what my inner child's view of women really is, now that I've gotten clear on what she thinks of men. My standard answer used to be, "I get along fine with women *and* men! I have friends of both sexes. Why would I have a problem with either one?"

But that's another lie I told myself because of the double bind I was forced into. Of course I feared men and imparted to them a set of characteristics in general to match my experience. Men were users, liars, and rapists. Why would they care about *my* needs?

Alongside that all-negative view of men, if I had assigned all negatives to females (as was pretty close to my experience through Mother), I think I would have felt absolutely rootless. The first gust of wind would have blown me away. It was easier to believe a lie about women . . . about my mother . . . that they were loving and supportive, spiritual, and generous. That they met the needs of children.

If you looked at her relationships with her women friends, my mother did fit much of that description. She could give all those qualities to her friends (codependently caretaking them), while withholding them from her family.

Mom never took her children seriously. We were "only kids." If she could convince herself we were less than human somehow, maybe she could feel less guilty about ignoring us.

I can remember an old cliché she used: "Just ignore her, she's only trying to get attention!" She never noticed the tragedy in it for me, the child who *needed* attention. She never gave it. My mental portrait of her shows her sitting frozen on the couch—separate, alone, staring into space.

How could she have been so blind to what she did to us? She pitted her children against each other. Each of us heard a recitation of our own faults and our siblings' strengths, designed to encourage our mutual resentment. Of course, it was every man for himself! Divide and conquer. Maybe she was afraid that if there was a bond among us, we'd have each other and she'd be left alone. As it was, somehow she won each child's reluctant allegiance to herself against the others.

First Timothy 5:8 says, "If anyone does not provide for his relatives, and especially for his immediate family, he has denied the faith and is worse than an unbeliever" (NIV). To say that Mother didn't provide for her family, emotionally anyway, is to put it mildly. We were pretty effectively abandoned, while she raised up a scorpion in our midst—Gary—and forbade us to defend ourselves against it! All the while mouthing "Christian" platitudes.

She took away every defense I had and enabled Gary to use me in any way, shutting her eyes to it. Why couldn't she protect her daughters? We never hurt her. Was she seeing some female characteristic in us that she rejected for her own reasons?

Did she have a warped view of women that corresponded to my view of men? Or was it that the male prototype she projected onto Gary was so strong that her daughters were insignificant? The relative favor she bestowed on us certainly wasn't dependent on our behavior. There had to be some other reason within *her*.

Whatever pain she carried didn't take away her adult responsibility to her children. She abandoned me. I've carried guilt and shame all my life that rightfully belonged to her. I lay down the burden at her feet.

Isaiah 49:15–16 is for me: "Can a mother forget the baby at her breast and have no compassion on the child she has borne? *Though she may forget* (italics mine), I will not forget you! See, I have engraved you on the palms of my hands; your walls are ever before me" (NIV).

My mother may have forgotten me, but the Lord has not.

Thursday, October 26, 1:00 A.M.

I had the feeling you needed to talk to me. Are you upset?

Just sad and quiet. I'm glad somebody finally listens.

Nobody ever listened to you before, did they?

No, they never thought I had anything important to say. I needed Mama to listen, but she was always so busy with her own problems, she didn't want to hear mine. She said "Kids don't have problems! Just wait till you grow up and find out how hard life really is!" How could she say that? I was being raped all those years. I was so alone and afraid. And anyway, Mama would have said I was bad if she knew.

Don't you think she must have known what Gary was doing?

I don't know. She never noticed anything. Wouldn't she have yelled at me if she knew?

Maybe it was easier for her to pretend she didn't know so she wouldn't have to think about it . . . and feel guilty.

Guilty? Why would she feel guilty? It was me that was having sex when I wasn't supposed to. I was the one being nasty.

Maybe she would have felt guilty because mothers are supposed to protect their little girls from people who would hurt them. Like Gary. She already knew he molested that other little girl in the neighborhood.

But she never believed that about Gary! She always took his side, always believed whatever he said, even though he lied all the time. I never understood how she could love him and reject me, when I always tried to be good. There was nothing I could do to make her love me. She only loved him.

Maybe it was because she loved Gary that she ignored his molesting you. Maybe she couldn't face the fact that he was being so bad.

Yeah. That was more important to her than protecting me.

Mama didn't know how to protect you. But God was there. Yesterday I found a passage in the Bible that tells how God protected you . . . even from the beginning:

"Yet You brought me out of the womb; You made me trust in You even at my mother's breast. From birth I was cast upon You; from my mother's womb You have been my God. Do not be far from me, for trouble is near and there is no one to help" (Ps. 22:9–11 NIV).

judy even when there was no one to help and you thought you were all alone, God was there. Like Jan Frank said in *A Door of Hope,* God sees the end from the beginning. He knew you would be healed. And I can protect you now. It's going to be all right.

Saturday, October 28, 2:30 A.M.

Yesterday afternoon I prayed for some insight to help me understand Mom. I was drowning in a whirlpool of bitterness about how she abandoned me to Gary.

Awake at this hour, maybe God has something to show me. So here I am with pen in hand, ready to take down the message. Why, God? I need to understand—why didn't she protect me?

Is there any simple answer? I can't know my mother's heart. She is who she is because of her own set of experiences and the choices she made in response to them. But her choices hurt me.

When she was just sixteen she chose to marry my father, Jack—an angry, violent man, who beat us and abandoned us, with never a Christmas card ever after. She was a victim to Jack. I don't remember much about Martin, the man she chose as my first stepfather, except we weren't happy. Then she chose Richard, whose raging tirades hurt me just as much as his fists would have. She was, and is, a victim to Richard. She always chose abusive men.

She chose to turn her back on Gary's abuse of me. He turned out just like Jack. Did Mom's inner child see herself as a victim to Gary, just because of his gender?

Did she see herself as a victim to all males? Did she have a skewed image of men's attributes that matched mine, and an inability to say no that matched my own flattened boundaries? Was my mother a victim of childhood sexual abuse too? Did someone teach her early on that women *have* no other choices?

I don't have the answer to that question. But I have that mental image of my mother slumped frozen on the couch, staring into space. She was dissociated! Dissociation is a form of emotionally separating yourself from a reality that is a source of pain, and it's a major effect of traumatic childhood experience. Her mind was somewhere else.

The very picture of helplessness and hopelessness, numbed by tranquilizers, she sat on that sagging couch in that filthy house, surrounded by the litter of a life gone terribly wrong, and she emotionally ran away. All her hopes to be an artist and a teacher were stymied by the urgent necessity of just keeping her head above water, surviving the abuse of the men in her life by trying not to feel her pain.

From my reading I know statistics say that incest is commonly a multi-generational chain. One study said 90 percent of mothers of incest victims are themselves victims. The common effects of sexual abuse—multiple sexual relationships, inappropriate choice of partners, obesity, ulcers, drug or alcohol abuse, gynecological problems, hysterectomies, headaches, low self-esteem, emotional detachment, dissociation, chronic depression, chronic rage—all fit my mother.

Suddenly I know to the depths of my being that my mother was somehow a victim very much like me. This knowledge isn't given to me to accuse her, or to convince a jury, but simply to create a space in my own heart to understand what terrible pain and shame she carried! Her inability to be a parent makes perfect sense. She was helpless to stop Gary. She defended him because he was male and that automatically made him powerful. Females are bad. Daughters can't be protected. There is no way to stop what is going to happen anyway.

How very sad her life has been. And how dramatically my feelings have changed as I have written this journal entry! I can feel compassion for her. An answer to prayer?

Sitting here just now, surprisingly engulfed in a sense of euphoric peace I have never known before, I was thinking how God has guided and shaped my life to bring me to this time of healing . . . this moment when it is suddenly right to forgive my mother.

Then I heard what I have never believed in before. God's voice. Not audibly, but words showing up in my head, unbidden. Words that don't fit my current self-concept. They came from outside myself. In the silence, came the words:

"This is my beloved daughter, in whom I am well pleased. I purchased you with the life of my perfect Son, and you are worth the price."

I am valued! To a degree that takes my breath away. God loves me. I don't understand the timing of this message, but oh, how much I can believe in healing now! I have heard His voice.

Wednesday, November 1, 11:30 P.M.

Jason's response this afternoon wasn't exactly what I expected, when I shared my processing about my mother with him. Oh, he agreed with the probability of my assessment of Mom's experience. And he rejoiced with me over hearing God's voice. He believed it.

What surprised me is that he didn't seem to share my enthusiasm for forgiving her right now. Isn't forgiveness what we're working toward? Isn't that what I'm *supposed* to do?

What he said was, "Let's take our time and make very sure the wound is clean before we rush to seal it over again."

Does he think there's *more* to work on in there? I can't think of anything else. After all we've dredged up, surely I'm close to being finished, aren't I? I am *tired* of being in the middle of this painful mess. I want it to be over. I want to keep feeling that peace I was given the other night.

Okay, maybe I *am* rushing to be finished. I guess, given my very faulty memory of my childhood, there could be something else back there in the black hole of my past that needs healing. I just don't *want* there to be anything else.

Sunday, November 5, 3:00 A.M.

Is it possible Jason is wrong? Oh, maybe there is more to work on, maybe I'm not finished with my feelings about Mom. But couldn't he be wrong that this forgiveness of my mother is premature? It still feels very right. But Jason has more objectivity. And he's been through this before with other counselees. Maybe it isn't real. How do I know? I don't.

Whether it's real or not, *judy* still has to grieve the loss. *judy* and I together wrote another poem, from our new understanding of Mama. I wish I could share it with her, but I'm not healthy enough to be with her without getting sucked back into the old family system again. I have to be separate until I'm stronger. I wish I knew how to love her. I wish she knew how to love me.

MOTHER,

I never knew the secrets bound
And locked away inside your soul.
Your barricades of fear around
The panic of not being whole
Rose to the sky, and kept me out.
No entrance to your vault of shame,
Without a sentry's piercing shout,
Allowed a glimpse of your old pain.
Denial mortared bricks of blame.
They made a fortress barbed with lies.
Your hate, in sheets of bitter rain
Concealed the noise of desperate cries . . .
To save your trembling inner child
Who longed to hear a lullaby,
To see a reassuring smile,
To feel safe arms, give shuddered sigh.
To rest. Exhausted eyes to close.
To trust in others to protect
Her innocence in soft repose.
To know that harm would not molest.

My grief is for our shared despair
That could have lifted, if we knew

Just how to bear the risk, and care.
Your secret nightmares were mine, too.
We could have held each other's pain,
Drawn strength, and hope, and felt at home.
And walked together free of shame.
But I must journey on alone.

CHAPTER 7

My Brother Wasn't the Only One!

No matter how much drama I experienced, there was no quick cure. I got just enough grace to get through each day. Grief surrounded me, weighing me down, but in its midst I received moments of reassurance that buoyed me up.

It took me so long to learn to consistently depend on God. The Lord knew I still had a lot to learn about trusting Him to answer my prayers about my daily pain. I still needed Jason to lead me through the steps to getting God's attention. I still unconsciously believed that a man had to be the one praying for me—because females aren't worthy of God's attention.

Tuesday, November 7, 11:00 P.M.

Another memory showed up unbidden yesterday. I had called Carla again, and one of her comments reminded me of the time Gary enlarged a crack in the plastered shower wall, chipping a hole all the way through to the closet in his room. Pervert! Here's one time Mom knew what he was doing. She made him patch the plaster. But how long was it there before he fixed it? How many times did he watch me? And Carla? And Mom?

After hanging up the phone, my feelings of disgust grew into a full-blown panic attack. Yes, I finally admit to panic attacks. There is no other explanation for my sudden fear and rapid pulse. I felt as if I had just narrowly escaped a head-on collision with a school bus full of first-graders, amid squealing brakes and the terrorized screams of children. I had the same adrenaline rush.

That anxiety was prompted by the memory of a time Gary used that hole in the wall to look at me with my knowledge. I was following his orders, but the feelings of shame that overwhelmed me in remembering the event were telling me, *It's your fault! He wasn't physically forcing you. Why didn't you run out of the room?* Over and over the guilt assailed me.

It wasn't until my session with Jason today that I had any relief from that feeling. This time I didn't resist going *back there* the way I had before. I hated the idea, but I knew saying the words would take away the pain.

So my inner child recounted the whole shameful incident, and Jesus was listening there with my counselor. Jesus filled the hole in the plaster with softened soap, and when He finished, it was as if the wall had never been damaged. After *judy* was dressed, she and Jesus both forgave Gary for what had just happened. Hard as it was, I forgave myself, too.

Then He led *judy* outside into the daylight. He took off His sandals and climbed her tree with her in the front yard. It was the safest place she had.

Sitting on that branch with Jesus beside her, she knew that whatever is hidden in her darkened memory, however shameful it is, God will remember her sins no more.

Maybe I will still have memories I have to talk about in therapy, but I *can* know how much healing there is waiting for me when I'm ready.

Sunday, November 12, 1:45 A.M.

Memory loss (which I never would have admitted before) is something society snickers at. Redundant soap opera plots. Fakery. The image comes to mind of the old "I Love Lucy" episode when Lucy tries to put one over on Ricky. She glides slowly across the room, ghost-like, eyes wide and blank as she coos, "Who am I? What am I? Where am I?" Oh, no, amnesia! Ricky falls for it again.

Real repression of memory is more like when a six-year-old looks for his missing shoe. "Have you checked in your closet?"

He explodes, "Yes, and it's not there! I'll never find it!"

So the parent walks into the child's room, opens the closet door, and surveys the piles of fallen toys and clothes littering the floor. The first item the parent picks up is a discarded jacket, and underneath, to the surprise of nobody but the six-year-old, is the lost shoe.

Without any willingness to find unpleasant memories, they will hide forever under strategically placed clutter. But even unremembered, their presence is felt, like hidden chunks of Kryptonite slowly sapping Superman's strength.

He doesn't have to see them to be poisoned by them. Denial is no help.

So here, in the middle of the night, is another memory. Are these memories showing up because I feel safer in believing there is some power that will defuse them rather than let them destroy me? I think *judy* knows exposing them to the light is her only hope. At last she's willing to risk finding the memories she tucked away so long ago, even though it still hurts to look.

I remembered my favorite uncle, Hank, who married my mother's younger sister. I used to visit their house on my way home from school. Hank was a mailman, home early in the day and always happy to see me. Nobody yelled at their house, so I enjoyed being there.

What triggered this memory? Unexpectedly, I thought of a fragment of a conversation with Hank. We were at Grandma's house, just the two of us talking on the porch. He made a pun, playing on the word *balls*. He meant *testicles*. Staring at him blankly, I felt fear.

How does this comment fit with the fact that my uncle was a respected man, a deacon in the church? Why would he be telling dirty jokes to a little girl of ... what ... eight or ten years old? The only reason I can find is that he must have abused me, too. A memory of that incident will show up in its own time. In the meantime, *I know*.

Exploring Hank's life, I can find some puzzle pieces to confirm the dark side of his character. The hidden side. Maybe the most obvious piece is that he married into what looks to be an incestuous family system. He spoke the same language or he wouldn't have been attracted.

He was killed in an accident ten years ago. After the funeral, I spoke some words of consolation to my aunt, his widow. Her face turned darkly animated, angry. She said, "Oh, if you only knew what he was really like!" Then she burst into tears. "But if I could only have him back, I wouldn't care!" Maybe at the time I wasn't consciously aware that I *did* know what Hank was like.

Oh, here's another piece. Was it Mom who told me—or maybe Hank himself—that he had had affairs with women on his mail route? It wasn't just a couple of affairs either. Many! Yeah, that jibes with the uncle I knew. He was a popular guy—witty, fun-loving, athletic. He could charm ladies. And he had access to a lot of them.

As he had access to several nieces. Jason has told me that child abusers, like men who repeatedly have affairs, are often sex addicts. It's a compulsion. A sickness.

It makes me sick, too. I feel ill.

Saturday, November 18, 8:00 P.M.

Today we took the girls to an afternoon movie, then went to a restaurant for hamburgers. It was one of those days when the light of my healing broke through the heavy clouds that darken my spirit. I was feeling pretty good, able to focus on the kids and David, instead of obsessing on incest, which is more standard for my state of mind lately.

Then came the memory. We had just sat down at the table with our food, when a brick wall collapsed on top of me. I was suffocating, and I certainly couldn't eat or converse with the children. I gripped David's arm.

"What is it?" he asked.

"A flashback," I forced out.

I stared at the table, willing myself to breathe. Inhale. Exhale. Inhale. Exhale. Grit your teeth and get through this second. Then the next second. Don't look at the picture that just exploded onto the screen in your head. Don't listen to the pounding surf that is only your own pulse beating against your eardrums. Just breathe.

I huddled in the car on the way home, holding myself rigid and biting my lip to keep from shrieking at the kids tussling in the backseat. David cajoled and finally threatened them to quiet their bickering. My throat ached. Just breathe.

My old survival style is the one I'm still using. I have to get away from everybody. There is no safety except in solitude. Even alone, the fear does not go away. But it is unbearable to be in the same room with anyone else, to be forced to process any human input when the circuits are already screaming from the overload.

Finally behind closed doors in my bedroom, I groped for the only lifeline I knew. I called Jason's answering service and had him paged.

"I have this horrible feeling and I don't know what to do with it!" I said when he returned my call.

"Tell me what's happening," he answered calmly.

"I remembered . . . about my uncle!" Could he make sense of that? My mouth would not form words any more clearly.

"Okay. Let's concentrate on just getting through the weekend until I see you on Monday."

"Isn't there something to kill this picture in my head?"

"It probably wouldn't be a good idea to go out and get drunk. Better stay close to home." Easy for him to say.

"So all I have to get through this weekend is hot tea and aspirin?" *I'm drowning and I have to tread water till Monday!*

"Writing seems to have helped you get through some other difficult times. Why don't you try that now?"

"Yeah. But it never hurt this much before. I keep thinking . . . I've been looking for this memory to show up. Maybe it never really happened. Maybe I made it up to fit what I was looking for."

"What have we already said about that?"

I sighed and recited, "Nobody makes up something so painful. It's real or the feelings wouldn't accompany the picture. But, Jason, you know how creative I am!"

"Yes. But even creative people do not make up a history that would cause this kind of trauma. It happened. Not because of you, but because your uncle was a sick man who took advantage of an innocent child."

How many times does he have to say the same thing over again? When is my inner child going to believe in the innocence Jason perceives? She hears the words Jason uses to reassure her and the words I offer to soothe her in the middle of the night, but with each new memory, she is still caught in that whirlpool of shame. She's drowning in it.

A ten-minute phone conversation with a therapist is at best an inflatable giraffe swim ring, which might look pretty good to hang onto in a wading pool. But I am surrounded by angry waves in an endless ocean. I can't see the shore, and I can't feel the bottom, and God seems very far away right now.

Jason trusts me to be able to survive this flashback without him. I don't feel that strong. But I don't have many options. I think I'll go for a walk. The walls are closing in.

Sunday, November 19, 10:45 P.M.

Walking yesterday helped just a little to alleviate the stress I was (and still am) feeling. Today when I went out to walk, I felt as if I were going to explode, like a pressure cooker all steamed up with no escape valve. So after a block I began to run, working to stress my body instead of my emotions. I ran a half mile, remembering the satisfaction I used to find in physical depletion when I was jogging regularly eight years ago.

It reminded me of the fact that so many incest victims are self-destructive. I can feel the same agony that makes some of us burn ourselves or slash our wrists, even when we don't acknowledge suicidal feelings.

It comes from that unbearable pressure inside us. We're all swollen up and ready to burst from the lifetime of secrets stuffed down behind our conscious memory. Like the taut hardness of a nine-and-a-half-month pregnant belly, the surface of our lives is stretched to cover that huge mass of lies and shame. Isn't there a way to release the pressure before we explode into a million unrecognizable pieces? Cutting wrists might be, for some of us, a misdirected effort at self-preservation, an attempt to create a controlled outlet to vent the steam that threatens to split us wide open.

Exercise is a safer steam valve. Some recovering victims use dance or karate or aerobics. Let the energy from the emotional pain fuel movement. That's how running felt. Like directing the pressure through a hose to run an engine, instead of rupturing the surface and spewing in every direction. It helped some.

This is still a miserable weekend. *God, give me strength.*

Monday, November 20

My session with Jason released a whole lot of pressure this afternoon. I pulled myself together, panic attack and all, and said the words for what happened.

Hank must have just returned from Germany. He left my aunt at home soon after they were married, while he was gone for a two-year tour of duty in the army. His stint in Germany would have been a perfect opportunity for him to have indulged his sexual addiction, wouldn't it?

Back home, there was a family fish fry at our house, to welcome him. This was the only time I ever remember having guests at home. I was seven years old ... before Mom married Richard ... before Gary!

In the midst of all the noise and talking that was going on in the front yard, Hank took me into the backyard.

"But that doesn't make any sense!" I told Jason. "It couldn't have happened that way. Even a sex addict would be smarter than to molest a little girl around the back corner of the house when the family was gathered in the front yard!"

"Not necessarily," Jason answered. "Imminent danger is a source of a 'high' for a sex addict. And in your family, if someone *had* walked in on what was happening, would they have raised an alarm? Would they have protected you? Or would they have disbelieved what they saw and kept quiet?"

I suppressed a moan. "I guess they would have pretended it didn't happen. Mom never allowed herself to believe what she had to know about Gary. My value wasn't high enough for anyone to raise a fuss. Men are more important."

It was real, as much as I longed to believe it was all a lie. And I couldn't avoid it anymore. But Jason was with me as *judy* went back to that sunny afternoon and faced what happened.

She broke the silence of thirty years of keeping the secret. For the first time, she told how Hank had spoken softly to her and taken down her summer shorts, and touched her . . . with his hands and with his mouth. With his tongue.

Right there in the open yard, against the back wall of the house, by the rosebushes. Just around the corner of the house was the swing set where *judy* spent so many hours alone, swinging endlessly, singing songs to herself she made up as she went along. Trying so hard just to be a child.

But now Jesus was with her. He stopped what Hank was doing and let her cover herself. He healed her shame with forgiveness and compassion. He led her away. Then Jesus held her and comforted her as she cried.

It doesn't hurt quite as much as it did before.

Wednesday, November 22, 11:45 P.M.

We've changed to three sessions of therapy per week for a while. I need that much support right now. All week I'm treading water, trying to keep my chin above the waves so I don't drown. Therapy sessions are life rafts I can hang onto for a little while, before I plunge back into the water on my own. But I'm so tired. I need those rafts closer together.

Jason raised the question today of the possibility that in the scene with Hank I might have experienced an orgasm— (*Oh, this is so hard to write down! I don't want it to be true, but I'm afraid—*).

I'll start again. He said perhaps I was taken by surprise by the feelings I couldn't identify and thought I was going to die. I read somewhere that a French slang phrase for orgasm is *le petit mort*, meaning the little death."

Well, a seven-year-old child wouldn't know what orgasm was and would have been overwhelmed and frightened by the intensity of it. And, yes, the books say that orgasm is possible at a very early age—even toddlerhood.

But I resist the idea of being surprised by a sexual climax. Orgasm, for me, has always been an effort of will and concentration. Never something that could have sneaked up on me unaware! Is that only because of my sexual damage? Maybe I should ask *judy*.

Sweetheart, can you tell me about the feelings you had when Hank was touching you?

I didn't want him to!

I know. He took advantage of you, honey, and there's no way you could have stopped him. But the feelings he made you have . . . you couldn't help them, but they had to feel nice.

I was scared! I didn't want him to do that to me. It was bad! He made me bad!

No. It wasn't your fault. You weren't bad. It wasn't your fault. It wasn't your fault. . . . I am rocking myself even as I scribble these words and weep with her.

I feel like a voyeur trying to see back inside my own memory! Asking myself—her—those questions is abusing her all over again. She doesn't want to remember because it was too shameful. I don't have to make her remember.

But I know anyway. The whole memory of that time with Hank is focused on his effort to stimulate *me*. He never asked me to touch him, because his excitement came from the power he had over a female of any age—the "high" of controlling her at the deepest level. Making her want that feeling.

I'd rather he'd have held a knife to my throat! Maybe I wouldn't have felt so responsible. I'm sure he told himself he was doing me a kindness. Making me feel good. That this wasn't abuse, it was a tender introduction to loving.

Ha! The truth is, even the gentlest of abuse is *still* abuse, and the child is violently stripped of her self-control. It's just another rape. Love has nothing to do with it. She is humiliated in the most agonizing way, because she has to hate herself for the badness he introduced her to.

No wonder this memory hurt so much. It's still painful even after the healing I received. Because it brought me face to face with my inability to prevent my own frightening pleasure. I never asked for it. He forced it on me because there was no way to say no to it. I was *not* responsible! But *judy* doesn't believe it yet. Poor child.

judy has been trying to prevent orgasm during my whole marriage—disconnecting the wires to eliminate several paths altogether, and making sure the other lines are faulty. And then there's the depression, because I am *bad*.

To be able to admit this memory now, along with what it means, is a sign that *judy* feels safe with the adult me and safe with Jason. Is there any greater shame than the pleasure? But *she* had enough courage to face it. It is healing.

Thursday, November 23, 11:00 P.M.

It hurts to know that I was a victim to more than one person. Jason says it's very common, once personal boundaries are damaged, to be abused by several people. Abusers must have radar that picks out victims who can't resist them because they don't know how. I was taught to be afraid of *all* men.

This afternoon I was thinking about my fear of Richard. I remembered a time, after Carla had left home—I must have been seventeen—that Richard came into my room while I was lying on my bed reading. He walked in without warning, and was suddenly, startlingly, standing over me. I stared hard at my book. He sat down on the edge of my bed, and without a word, leaned over and gave me an awkward kiss on the cheek. Rigid with hate and fear, I held my breath and fixed my eyes unflinchingly on the page, willing him to go away, but unable to speak.

After a minute, he stood and walked out of my room, leaving me shaking. My experience with men told me he was about to be sexual with me. Was I misinterpreting his intentions, expecting to be treated as the others had treated me? Was I right about his intentions but successful in repelling his approach with only stony silence? I don't know. For whatever reason, he left the room. At least that was one time it didn't happen. Was I really wrong about Richard all along?

Friday, November 24, 2:00 A.M.

Jason asked me to do a diagram of the house I was raised in. My first reaction was revulsion. I couldn't have explained why the idea bothered me so much, but now that I've finally done the drawing, I can understand.

A diagram of the house is specific, so I can't avoid seeing some very disturbing reminders. Like the fact that my bedroom had no door! No boundaries. Privacy was nonexistent. (Your room, your possessions, your body is not your own. Do not withhold any of it from anyone who wants it.)

Until Carla left to get married as soon as she was of legal age, she and I shared a room that was an addition to the back of the house. Actually there were two rooms, separated by a partition. Closer to the rest of the house, the first room was used for sewing and junk piled everywhere. There was no framework for a door to be hung in the doorway between the two rooms. And no door from the sewing room into the hall. Just an opening. Like an invitation.

I drew Gary's room, with the closet where he watched me in the adjoining bathroom. The kitchen where there was no birthday cake. The backyard with the swing set and the corner where Hank took advantage of me.

But there was more. I drew the row of cedars that formed a giant hedge fifteen feet across (we called them "The Bushes"), between our property and the neighbor to the west. We weren't allowed to play in them . . . there might be snakes or something. But Gary used his machete to hack out tunnels through them. I have the feeling that the only snake in those bushes was Gary. *Something* bad happened in there.

The house was on an extra large lot for "privacy," which meant the neighbors couldn't hear the yelling so easily. Sketching in the fence that separated our house from the neighbors on the east brought to mind their son Dennis, who was strange. He was years older, yet he befriended Gary. That's not enough evidence to prove that he was strange. Is there something else about him? The thought doesn't go away. There's something. . . .

Monday, November 27, 2:00 A.M.

Another bomb just went off. Here I am again, faced with a flashback that has me shaking with panic. I'll be with Jason this afternoon, and we'll ask God for healing. But in the meantime, I have to get through the hours. I have to write it down. It's Dennis, the neighbor. . . .

God, help me with this! I'm so afraid! I can't make the words go on the paper. Why is there so much *fear?* I was never violently abused. Nobody ever beat me. I have not felt any memories of physical pain.

My suffering through the magnitude of terror I am experiencing makes me shudder in empathy for the victims who lived through unimaginable agonies from sadistic abusers. It is no wonder that so many of them developed multiple personalities. What strength they had! To find a way, *any* way, to survive those horrors with all those parts of themselves set aside for the day they could find those parts and learn to love them. I'm in awe of their courage to exist through it.

My own fear rises in my throat and threatens to choke me. But I *will* survive it. I am *not* going to let my abusers win. So grit your teeth and write it down!

Dennis raped me. He didn't hold a knife, either. Kind words were enough for a twenty-year-old man to lure a ten-year-old child who was so starved for affection. It was still rape. No was not allowed.

The neighbor family was among those who were alarmist enough during the Cold War to build a bomb shelter in their backyard. Dennis, a ham radio enthusiast, invited me into the shelter to see the radio. The tour of the tiny living quarters included one of the beds.

I'm not even going to ask *judy*. All I can feel is the numbness. No pain. No pleasure. Just pressure. The weight of his body on top of mine. The shame! And the fear.

There is no way to know how many times it happened. With Dennis, with Hank, or with Gary. Certainly the memories I have are only representative of all the other times. But each time was the same despairing powerlessness. Hopelessness. Fear.

Monday, November 27, 10:30 P.M.

Thank God for the relief I feel after a memory healing session! It isn't Jason's power. He doesn't have any magic. I guess secular therapists get results with their clients, too, because God works for our good whether the therapist acknowledges the source of healing or not. "God heals, but the doctor takes the fee" said Benjamin Franklin. I'm grateful to have a Christian counselor who gives God most of the credit. Jason knows how to access the power source.

I think I see why the memory with Dennis was so powerful, and why fear has been such a strong element, even without physical pain. Knowing about Dennis establishes a *list*. I had almost forgotten about Leo when I was five; Hank, when I was seven; Gary when I was nine. Were there others? How many names are on that list? People who used this body I thought I knew. I was powerless to have stopped anyone.

Somehow the *badness* that *judy* shamed herself with is magnified with each name added to that list. *Couldn't I have stopped any of them?* she cries. No. Each time the terror of her absolute defenselessness was brand new.

Wednesday, November 29, 1:30 A.M.

Maybe I should give up and write more during the daytime. Would that mean I could sleep better at night? No, probably I would just end up finding something else to work on in the middle of the night.

Reading yet another book about sexual abuse (this one quite clinical) this afternoon, there was one sentence that hit home pretty hard. The book referred to another trend observed in survivors of incest. Apparently child victims frequently develop the habit of sleeping with one hand or foot free of the bedcovers.

I could never go to sleep when I was a kid unless I had one foot out from under the covers. Before therapy, I would have steadfastly maintained that it didn't mean anything.

The author of the book conjectured that victims who slept like that were seeking a way to have a part of themselves separate from what happened in the bed. It was an effort to withhold *something* from the total control the abusers exercised over their bodies.

I can believe that. It was as if I might hope that my right foot could say no to the possession and powerlessness, while the rest of my body could never find a way to prevent it.

Is there no end to the layers of hurt I keep peeling back, only to find more pain underneath? I *know* God is with me, or I couldn't exist through the overwhelming sorrow I continue to feel. But I want to be finished! How long am I going to hurt?

Friday, December 1, 2:15 A.M.

Another memory will show up sometime soon. I got just an edge of a picture of something. There's more to come.

This flashback is like a silent movie clip, in black and white. I see a hand, but there is no face. I can't make out who it is. Fingers, with meticulously groomed nails. Fingers in my vagina. There's another name on *the list*, but I don't know who it is!

I've used up all the adjectives for the grief and sadness I'm wallowing in. I'm so sick of it. But it isn't going to stop until everything shameful has been said. *God, give me strength. Can't I be finished?*

CHAPTER 8

Current Events

So many interlocking issues showed up all together. I couldn't separate them; I had to work on all of them at once. All the old ghosts roaming around in my head were very much current problems. The abuse didn't stop when I left my childhood home. I was still at the mercy of the shame which had been instilled in me.

The journal represented the progress I was making as I worked with Jason, but it never captured all the painful steps I took between entries. I know there were hundreds of little revelations I never wrote, and can't identify now. There was never a day without some new awareness. I never found a way to take a break from the process.

Saturday, December 2, 11:30 P.M.

Another reason I wake to write at night: Writing is processing the issues my counselor raises. I'm alone, figuring out and feeling the meaning of the puzzle pieces we're working on. My only safety as a child lay in being alone. Any time someone was with me, I was risking abuse.

Potential interruptions mean I'm not safe to feel the pain because it makes me vulnerable. In the middle of the night, there's less chance of interruption, so my inner child is safer.

As for the reason I'm awake on this particular night:

Last week David took our daughters out of school for a special afternoon together—shopping and dinner out. None of them had ever met my therapist, and both girls were curious about who I was spending all this time with. So they met me at the office. I introduced them all to Jason, and they talked for five minutes, then trooped out the door.

At home that evening, I asked David for his first impression of Jason. "He seems to be a non-threatening kind of guy, which I guess is a good thing for a therapist to be."

I responded instantly in defense of my counselor. "I don't know, I can imagine that Jason might be kind of sexy under other circumstances."

David shot me a very puzzled look, but said nothing.

Just now, I finally *heard* what I said! Here is more evidence of how very messed up my brain is! How confused!

I automatically equated the word *nonthreatening* with the meaning "nonsexual." Conversely, I must have the word *threatening* equated with "sexual." There's a whole unconscious dictionary down inside me that contains the meanings

114

of words the way they were back then. Where did I learn that threatening means sexual? From every male who used me!

If you met Gary today, you'd consider him a threatening person, all right. He was already a threatening person when I was a little girl. He taught me that threats and sex were automatically linked.

So why am I always attracted to nonthreatening kinds of men? I *like* men who are intelligent and gentle and kind, men who listen well and have a sense of humor. My husband is like that. Jason's like that. Every other man I've ever been attracted to is like that. If my inner child thinks nonthreatening men are nonsexual, why am I drawn to men I perceive as nonsexual?

Because my inner child doesn't want sex to be demanded of her. She hopes a nonthreatening, nonsexual man will be safe. Of course, my nonthreatening David *is* definitely a sexual person. So that didn't work out.

What about women who are attracted to men who *would* be perceived as threatening? Like Sylvester Stallone and Jack Nicholson. Those macho, "I'm gonna be rough on you 'cause I know that's the way you like it, baby" kind of guys. Look at all the women who find themselves in one relationship after another with abusive men! Show them a safer William Hurt or a James Garner kind of man and they'll say, "He's not my type!"

We incest victims seem to fall into two groups, but sometimes we switch groups. Group A says, "If you love me, you *won't* ask me for sex." Group B says, "If you love me, you *will* ask me for sex." Somebody scrambled our brains.

I switch groups depending on the situation, a maneuver which has been completely unconscious, but nonetheless very confusing to my husband. Somehow, whatever assumption he might make will probably be wrong for that occasion. Poor guy. Poor me, too. I haven't figured this one out yet.

Monday, December 4, 10:00 P.M.

We had yet another conversation about sex in my session today. My inner child resists the topic still, but I guess she hasn't got boundaries enough to refuse to talk about it. And I know I need to talk about it, or it won't ever get healed.

Jason brought up the topic of splitting. I used to think that word referred just to dissociating into multiple personalities. Of course, people with multiple personality disorder all have sexual abuse as a common denominator. That shows the depth of trauma from incest. Where do they get the word *disorder*, anyway? It seems to me that developing multiple personalities is probably the sanest, most creative coping mechanism they could have found to survive the violent hell they couldn't otherwise escape. The disorder existed in that crazy environment, not in the survivors.

Splitting can be less extreme, though. It's a way of dissociating by suddenly not being present to what's going on. Jason asked me where I *went* during the abuse, so as not to have to feel what was happening.

During the abuse, I went to the same place I still go sometimes when I space out in the middle of a conversation, or when I zone out and miss my freeway exit. I split to some other place inside my head. In the middle of making love, I find myself suddenly thinking of grocery shopping! So *that's* where that frustration comes from!

Some victims relate a sense of floating above themselves, watching what is happening to that little girl on the bed. I'm not conscious of ever watching myself in that way. My splitting was more like daydreaming. It was safer to be *anywhere* other than the part of my mind that was aware and feeling. I just disconnected. It got to be automatic.

So a large part of my sexual dysfunction comes from not being *able* to pay attention to sexual feelings. Pleasure felt dangerous because *judy* thinks pleasure makes her bad.

If she let herself feel arousal, she was painfully vulnerable to losing control in orgasm. Sex was something she couldn't prevent, so she tried her best not to be a part of it. Poor frightened child.

Tuesday, December 5, 3:00 A.M.

judy and I are awake again. For the last hour we've been venting grief about her damaged sexuality. Oh, the convolutions of her behavior that were forced in avoidance of pain!

We agonized over "splitting" in a poem:

> I was hollowed out.
> I left behind the flesh and feeling on my bed.
> Averted eyes so I could swear
> I never saw what happened there—
> What breathless gasps
> And silent screams
> And tearless eyes
> And tortured dreams
> Were stuffed behind my memory.

Thursday, December 7

At Jason's suggestion, I've been to several meetings of a twelve-step group for survivors of incest. It's based on the Alcoholics Anonymous program. My feelings about it are a tangle of conflicts. How do I decide if this is the group for me?

I've needed a group for a long time. For months I've been spilling my guts to assorted friends who don't have a clue as to how to respond to me. Their bewilderment has made me feel like a freak. I guess that's what Jason was concerned about when he said some people might not be safe to share with. So who *is* safe?

117

I need to hear other women's stories, to know I'm not weird. It has been a relief to be able to share my experiences in meetings without expecting a shocked response. No one has been shocked. All our histories have common threads of fear and pain and shame. One woman named Annie may get to be a friend. We have a bond that doesn't exist with people who had "normal" childhoods.

I was amazed at my first visit to see a group of fifteen grown women cuddling teddy bears. They have an assortment of stuffed animals for "loaners," or you can bring your own. It *has* affirmed the reality of the children inside us.

I'm getting less self-conscious about holding a "loaner" bear. Clutching a stuffed animal while we talk about such painful things is a surprising comfort to *judy*. A hurt little girl needs a friend to hang on to. I wish I'd had one back then. I don't remember ever having had a teddy bear as a child. Not that it should surprise me. But David was surprised that *anybody* could be raised without a teddy bear.

Yet I'm concerned that I'm hearing a lot of wallowing, and we aren't focusing on growth. Is anybody moving through their stuff, or are they planning on being hurt and angry forever?

And some of the stories scare me. It's easy to minimize my own pain when I hear the horrors some children have experienced. Jason has validated my trauma over and over. He cautions me not to deny its importance. There is no healing in denial.

Putting number values on individual suffering is pointless. Injuries need attention for healing to take place. Don't deny a wound its own pain value, just because there are greater hurts! There will always be greater hurts.

In learning to parent my inner child, I don't want to repeat Carla's mistake when she compared my suffering to Jesus' death on the cross. If I said to *judy*, "Come on, it wasn't that bad! Look at all the people who were hurt worse than you," I'd be continuing the same minimizing I've done all my life, and I'd short-circuit the healing process for my own *real* injury.

I'm still evaluating this group. Is this a question of boundary, to be able to protect myself? I wonder if this group isn't good for me, and I just don't recognize it because my boundaries are so screwed up. Would quitting be taking care of myself or being weak? I still need someplace safe to talk.

Sunday, December 10, 12:30 A.M.

I don't know why I even tried to go to sleep. In the middle of lovemaking, I had a mini-flashback. A sudden awareness of a recurrent feeling of anger.

I guess for years I've stuffed down reactions of anger at David for things he said or did to communicate that he wanted sex. I have never even identified it as anger, much less been able to recognize the source.

After eighteen years of marriage, the rut we're in is pretty deep. Both of us know what the expectations are, so why complicate the matter? One of us just locking the bedroom door is an obvious signal, like a command. If *I* lock the door, I must be raping him, because I'm responsible for sex. Bad *judy.*

If *David* locks the door, or gives any of the other signals I've memorized, then I feel as though he's summoning me to "assume the position." Prepare to be used. So I'm a helpless nine-year-old again, about to be raped. If that's what's been down inside me every time we've had sex all these years, it should come as no surprise that orgasm is difficult and often not worth the effort.

Even more painful, no matter how sweet David is being, if he smiles and says, "Why don't you come here and take that off?", I'm *hearing* an order. I'm a lamb led to slaughter, but at the same time, I'm flashing back to feeling responsible for what happened—I am choosing to take off my garments, walk to the bed (I am not being dragged, led, or carried), and have sex voluntarily!

judy cries out, *Don't make me responsible for what* you *want! I never asked for that burden! I just didn't know how to stop it. She's angry for being set up.*

How I envy women who don't have all these triggers rigged to every little innocent phrase and look associated with sex! Words and movements I haven't identified are still setting off alarms in my head, producing fear and anger in response to what happened back then. I'm feeling shame that has been submerged for twenty-five years.

Tuesday, December 12

I read my last entry aloud to Jason yesterday. Somehow that's easier than just saying it.

"How are you going to tell David?" he asked.

I knew that was coming. I had just refused to think about it.

So last night after dinner, I read the same entry again to my husband. I didn't know how to say it otherwise. It was a harrowing conversation for us both.

David interrupted me several times, obviously hurt by what I had written. He's always thought our sexual relationship was the strongest part of our marriage. The discussion was mostly reacting to each other with knee-jerk reflexes, and the rational dialogue quickly degenerated to angry accusations.

We both finally recognized how we were hurting each other and backed up to try and smooth over the damage. But I couldn't stop crying, and both of us were frustrated.

Finally David said, "Get your coat. We need to get out of the house." He wouldn't take no for an answer. He instructed the girls to watch TV and keep the door locked. And we left.

In the car he was quiet and tense as he drove. Yet he wasn't angry anymore. I tried to continue the conversation through my tears. It seemed to become more complicated rather than more clear as we struggled with the words. Who ever taught us to communicate, anyway?

Then he pulled into the parking lot of the nearby department store where I worked last Christmas.

"Come on," he said.

I was still crying. "Why? I'm a wreck! Don't make me go in there! I know half the people who work there!" I held his arm as he opened the door to get out of the car.

Still sitting, he shut the car door, turned back to me and began to cry himself. "I wanted to surprise you," he said. "I wanted to buy a teddy bear for your inner child."

So then I really broke down. We sat in the front seat and held each other for fifteen minutes, both of us sobbing. I have no idea who may have passed and stared at the couple having the nervous breakdown in the Chevy. I didn't care.

David wanted to comfort me. He wanted to show *judy* she was loved. He needed comfort himself, after the shock of seeing the best part of our faltering relationship suddenly exposed as a lie all these years.

At last we went inside and bought the most beautiful furry brown bear *judy* had ever seen. It didn't matter who noticed the tears in my eyes.

Wednesday, December 13, 2:00 A.M.

How easy it is to forget my blessings when I'm in the midst of pain! I'm blessed to have David, despite the distance that separates us most of the time. We still have moments that remind us of our possibilities. Our breakdown before buying

Bear was one of those moments. I still long for a more continuous bond.

When I first loved you,
I needed you to fill
That empty place
In my soul.
Relief.
Somebody cared.
We fit together!
You showed me
Sparkles and stars.
But I was afraid.
Your love was too much
For me to understand.
My fear coiled in on itself.
Where once our souls
Had touched
And held,
My panic hollowed out
An empty void between.
Cold, hard jabs
Were easier,
Safer,
Than trust.
We lost each other.
But still we had sparkles,
And sometimes stars—
Reminders of touching more
Than fingertips.
Inside, I cried out
To bring you back.
But my lips were smiling,
Saying, "Everything's okay."
I closed the lid,

Muffled the inner voice
That wanted to reach you.
Alone was more familiar.
Risk was too terrible
To face.
But now,
Someone else
Has helped me know myself.
Shown me I am
Strong enough
To trust,
To risk,
Even when it hurts.
I'm learning to fill
My own empty place.
I'm asking out loud.
Come back to me.
I want you
For who you are
Instead of
Who I'm not.
I'm learning
How to love,
Why to give,
What to receive.

We're blessed with
Sparkles and stars.
I'm grateful for that.
But I believe
We can also have
Crackling firelight,
Sunshine,
Moonbeams,

And candleglow.
Come back to me.

Thursday, December 14, 2:15 A.M.

I took Bear to my session yesterday afternoon. I was a little embarrassed to carry him into the office.

Jason didn't seem to think it was odd at all. "What's your bear's name?"

"He's just—Bear," I answered self-consciously.

"He?"

Why is Bear a "he"? "I don't know why, he just *is*."

Jason asked me if he could hold Bear and took him from me with an unexpected air of . . . reverence! I watched in amazement as he set him carefully on his knee, nestling the furry shoulders comfortably in the crook of his right arm. He cupped his hand around the sole of Bear's small foot and looked back to me for a moment, as if to include me in his interaction with Bear.

Then, as Jason began speaking solemnly to Bear, it gradually dawned on me that he was not holding a stuffed animal on his knee. He was holding my inner child, safe against him. He never touched her where little girls are afraid to be touched. He respected her. He treated her like she was a real person. And he never abused her trust.

Jason told my inner child how very fortunate she was to be welcomed into a family who would love her and take good care of her. He told her that she was safe and protected from harm. And that she would always be listened to and believed in.

Receiving Bear back into my arms, I also received my inner child, with a renewed awareness of her vulnerability. Somehow, the adult me has to develop the protective boundaries she was never allowed to have. That's still very hard for me. But awareness is the first step toward success in making a change. I *do* have determination going for me. That child has suffered enough. I *will* learn to keep her safe.

Saturday, December 16, 1:30 A.M.

God, show me my boundaries. Over and over, I see myself sliding past the guard rails I try to put up. Just before I started therapy, those months I was miserably caretaking Tina during her divorce only happened because I didn't have boundaries. I was so enmeshed with her that Tina's disaster became my own. I was living her life, while my needs and responsibilities were shoved out of sight, out of mind. I never knew how to say no to her. Was that Jason's first clue to the extent of damage to my boundaries? Did he wonder if I was an incest victim from the first?

Even now, I watch myself willingly making myself vulnerable when it isn't safe or protective of my needs. *I am powerless to create healthy boundaries for myself, Lord. I need some help with this one.*

I'm traveling to be with Carla after Christmas. I've been chasing after that relationship for months, seeing her as the last vestige of family I can hang on to. I desperately want a family.

She rarely asks me to stop talking about incest, because *her* boundaries are damaged. But she changes the subject. And she hasn't phoned me since I started therapy. I always call her. I know she backs away from talking about my therapy and old family stuff because it's painful for her. She's not ready to deal with her own pain yet. So how can she support me? I guess she can't.

But when I try to set up a boundary to withhold some of my private pain from her, to protect myself, I might as well try to be in control of my progress across an ice-covered pond while wearing high-heeled shoes. Maybe the laws of gravity and momentum are in control, but I'm sure not.

125

Carla can't help me with what I'm going through right now. So how can I be with her in person and *not* talk about it? *Help me out, God. I can't see where it's safe and where it's not, and I haven't got any brakes.*

Tuesday, December 19, 2:45 A.M.

Yesterday's session included another discussion about sex. I still hear, *Why does it have to be sex?* all the way to Jason's office. Going public on the topic of sexual pleasure is so shameful for *judy*.

I told Jason about the image I have of sexual pleasure making me just a bug under a magnifying glass—being observed, on display, when I am most vulnerable and powerless and out of control. Telling that to Jason I felt almost as if I were letting him watch, too. *He's another man!* How can I let him know all this about me?

Uh-oh. Here's another flash—a different kind. I just thought of a story David told me years ago, one that always gave me chills. David pooh-poohed my disgust, said I had no sense of humor. I never understood my reaction, until now.

One night when David was a teenager, as the story goes, his brother Greg excitedly beckoned for David to join him in the family laundry room. A fascinating performance had just begun. David and his brother knelt together to observe a large roach twitching in the middle of the floor. She lay on her back, wriggling her legs in the air (David pantomimes this part enthusiastically). She was bringing baby roaches into the world.

The two brothers cheered her on as she writhed in focused concentration, delivering each egg. There was a pause and hushed stillness for a moment as she gathered her strength for the next effort. Finally, under the amused encouragement

126

of David and Greg, she brought forth the last of her young and lay quietly exhausted.

Both brothers gleefully congratulated her on her efforts. Greg counted the eggs she had labored so hard to produce. Then David squashed the roach and her brood with his foot.

Funny story? It was to David. But it was a story that made me cringe, because it triggered a vision of myself as the bug on the floor. For the entertainment of males (their relative power over me made the size difference realistic), I put on a command sexual performance. My own pleasure—like the birthing process, a natural function intended in the design of the female body—was the subject of amusement. Not only did my abusers make me responsible for the abuse, they ridiculed me for my natural responses and then stepped on me. I was rejected and left for dead.

No wonder orgasm depressed me! No wonder *judy* set up so many barricades to pleasure. What deeper humiliation is there than that? Pleasure made me the object of scorn, when all I wanted was for someone to care about me. And none of them would admit to hurting me! They'd all say, "She *wanted* it! She asked for it!"

Of course, victims have tremendous conflict about sexuality! We were brainwashed. The shame our abusers carried was forcibly transferred to our shoulders. But I won't carry it anymore.

God! Please take away the shame.

Tuesday, December 19, 8:00 P.M.

I'm searching for a face to attach to the flashback that's been hanging around for nearly three weeks without resolution. The black-and-white image of a hand—fingers in my vagina. I still can't *see* who it is, but I know it's not Gary or Hank or Dennis. The name that comes up as a possibility is Richard. Richard pared his fingernails scrupulously, daily cleaning them with his pocketknife. It looks like Richard's hand.

I'm trying not to jump to any hasty conclusions, but I've been asking myself for months why I was always so afraid of him. I can't remember a time I *wasn't* afraid of his rage or his shouted profanity. Do I have to withdraw the tentative warming of my feelings about Richard?

Did he abuse me physically? Carla says he never hit either of us girls. Carla's always had a much softer attitude toward Richard than I have. She says she always knew he loved us; he just wasn't able to show it. I never knew he loved us, if he did.

I'm not so sure he never hit me. I remember watching him unbuckle his belt. Was it to hit Gary? I draw a blank.

Was Richard's emotional abuse enough to make me so afraid? He was tyrannical in so many ways. He never allowed me or Carla to baby-sit for anyone outside the family; he said one of the kids might choke to death and we'd be responsible! How's that for instilling self-confidence in us? Of course, we were responsible enough to baby-sit our younger brothers. Because it happened to be convenient for our parents. We were commodities to be used.

His decisions were arbitrary and unpredictable. If we asked for a privilege, he refused to answer until we came back and made a second request. He made us beg for the crumbs he doled out!

I submitted to his edicts because I was afraid to rebel. I had seen Mom pit herself against his rage. She was as loud and angry as he was, and she still never made any progress. What chance did I have? I never dared to raise my voice to him. I could hardly bear to look him in the eye. I felt powerless and weak in his presence. Richard was absolute ruler in the house.

What does it say about him that Richard was so compulsive about being clean? He was a prude about his body.

Summer and winter, he never went bare-chested. He always wore dress pants and black oxford shoes. Then how do I remember seeing his shrapnel scars—on his bare chest? Or were they on his back? And I remember his white boxer undershorts. Did he walk through the hall like that on his way to the bathroom? I don't know.

Does everybody's memory look like Swiss cheese? There's another gap I hadn't thought of before just now. My sixth-grade teacher was Mrs. Zimmerman. Except that I *know* Mr. Brooks was my sixth-grade teacher! School was my comfort zone, my only security, so why would I have a memory gap concerning anything about school? It was also in sixth grade that Mr. Brooks (or WAS it Mrs. Zimmerman?) gave me a D on my science notebook assignment. That doesn't fit my profile at school. I remember having a panic attack when I saw that grade. Was there something especially traumatic going on when I was in the sixth grade that made me blank out whole chunks of my life? What happened?

I hate looking behind me and seeing *nothing!* But forcing recall doesn't seem to work. I guess it'll show up when it's ready. In the meantime my short-term speculation that Richard was protective of me no longer seems workable. I feel queasy.

Wednesday, December 27, 11:00 P.M. (At Carla's house)

I think I'm getting the answer to my prayer for help with boundaries. I've been stubbornly resisting Jason's subtle suggestions that I might be talking too much for my own good. If ten people or a hundred people know I'm an incest victim, so what? If they are people I choose to tell, and I deem them safe, what's the harm?

But I just now saw how my willingness to share my story—to make myself vulnerable—is really my adult self failing to protect that frightened inner child. I'm trying to learn to parent her. But I'm abusing her if I'm exposing her shame to more than the minimum number of people.

It's like a gossipy mother using her child as a conversation piece: "You know, she's got the cutest birthmark on her bottom! Come here, honey, let me show Maxine!"

Once *judy's* shame is healed, and she can rest, safe inside me, it'll be okay to share. It'll blow the lid off the secrecy that perpetuates the cycle. But for now, it hurts her. And I promised not to do that. I continue to pray for a more constant awareness of where I need to set my boundaries.

God *is* showing me where to stop laying myself on the line. Even being with her in person, I'm not struggling so hard to draw Carla into my process. It feels surprisingly natural to let Carla stay in denial. That's where she is. That's the only place her pain will let her be. She's afraid. Knowing what that feels like, I can give her space to deny everything during this visit. So I'm backing off.

I'm also backing off from Mom and Richard. I sent a Christmas gift for Mom, although I think now I need to break contact for a while. Several months ago I agreed with Carla to pay half the cost of a gift for Richard. That was when I was feeling more positive about him. But now the idea of giving him *anything* makes me nauseous.

Today I told Carla to sign the card and send it for us both; I would honor my commitment, but I didn't want to be any more involved than that.

"I thought you had changed your feelings about Richard," Carla said, "that you appreciated him more."

I answered, "Well, I *had* changed, but that was before I realized Richard must have raped me, too."

Carla turned to look me full in the face. "No."

End of conversation. I shrugged and let the matter drop. I didn't try to convince her or defend myself or explain. I let her think whatever she wanted to think. That feels like a boundary. It's growth. But it's hard to see her move to the other side of the fence. She's another loss, and I don't want to lose her.

So the rest of our visit will be filled with superficial conversation, instead of communication. I should have expected it. The important things, the painful things I need to say to her are too dangerous for her to hear yet. Maybe someday she will hear them.

Dwight Wolter, in *A Life Worth Waiting For*, said, "Cold hearts are hereditary." True. Carla doesn't mean to withdraw from me. She wants to love me, like I want to love her. But she's still bound up in the family chain of cold hearts—not genetic, but inbred all the same. Nobody ever taught us how to love.

I need a sister. I hope we'll find a healthy connection later on. In the meantime, I feel very much alone, even while I'm with her.

Lord, only You know Carla's needs, even better than she knows them. Take away her numbness. Let her feel her old pain. Give her the strength to face her losses, to be healed of her wounds. As You promised in Ezekiel 36:26, and as You have done in my life, remove the heart of stone that has burdened her. Give her a heart of flesh to know You.

I trust in Your mercy to offer her Your best, painful though it may be. Love her, God. Teach us to love each other.

CHAPTER 9

Declaration of Independence

Winston Churchill once said, "Dictators ride to and fro on the backs of tigers which they dare not dismount. And the tigers are getting hungry." I used to think of my parents as those dictators mounted on tigers who were their children. Perhaps the better analogy is that I had been the dictator—riding the rage I pretended was a pony. I tried to force it into conformity with what was expected of Christians. But the tiger could never be a pony. Its snarls were manifested in my lifelong outbursts of "temper". Eventually it was hungry enough to fully assert its real nature.

The only way to appease the tiger was to acknowledge its stripes, and set it free. It took an honest and specific admission of the <u>original</u> anger to defuse that volatile core of hatred. I wasn't creating new anger, only getting honest enough to confess the true emotions I had held inside all along.

Monday, January 1, 3:00 A.M.

Starting a brand-new year never seemed important to me before. This year feels different. For the first time in my life, the idea of a new beginning seems real. I have hope. Hopelessness has permeated the very air I've breathed all my life, until now. Even so, I could never have admitted it. Hopelessness, like depression, meant craziness. It was too shameful to concede. Another old family lie.

My load of shame is considerably lighter now than it was a year ago. I have joy in increasing measure, but I still hurt. Over and over I hear *judy*, at odd times, saying, *Jason* knows! *He* knows *all those* bad, *sexual things about me! Why does it have to be sex?"*

With her voice in my head, I go right into those feelings of shame and panic. So I have to be the parent again and tell her that it isn't her fault, that Jason doesn't think she's bad. And that I don't think she's bad.

That old shame goes hand in hand with isolation. I need to know I'm not alone. I still need to know that other women have the same shame, the same struggles. I need to talk about it.

The twelve-step support group filled some of that need, but that particular group wasn't working on the "steps", they were just sharing stories. There was no therapist to help us stay focused on growth. I had trouble avoiding codependency with some of the women there who weren't in therapy. They were looking for a caretaker like me. I can't rescue anybody else now. My own pain still consumes all my energy. I decided I didn't feel safe with that group, that it was okay to draw a boundary. So I quit.

But I did get to be friends with Annie. She's a Christian, too, and going out for coffee and dessert each week after the meetings, we discovered we have a lot of other things in common. We have similar family histories.

Annie called to invite me to a new therapy group her counselor is beginning next week. I've decided to join, and back off to twice a week with Jason. One of the benefits of a group is supposed to be that of experiencing a new "family" to fill some of the gap left by the loss of family of origin. I could use a family.

Wednesday, January 10, 11:00 P.M.

Last night was our first group therapy session. There were eight survivors of incest, plus Helen, the therapist.

Helen has been counseling for only a couple of years. She works within a government-subsidized agency to counsel victims of sexual assault. From what Annie has told me of her therapy, I can see that Helen has helped Annie make some good progress.

Yet Helen has some different views from Jason. I'm not used to the way she works. Helen isn't Jason, and I have to trust her to be the individual she is. Let go of control, Judy. God is in charge there, too, whether Helen knows it or not.

Most of our time last night was taken up with sharing our histories, punctuated with a lot of painful silence. I've loosened up a great deal about what I feel safe in saying. Of course, my boundaries have always been ground-level, anyway. So I shared quite a bit. I have to watch myself so I don't take over. It's a way I stay in control.

Maybe it's even harder for victims who responded to abuse by walling themselves inside impenetrable boundaries. Several group members are still where I spent a whole

135

lot of time—just trying to make the words come out. Or maybe they're afraid to try.

From the words that *did* come out, I can see that, despite the different details of our histories, we have so much in common.

Consuela, only nineteen, is the youngest. She's preparing for the upcoming criminal prosecution of her father for sexual abuse. He made her pregnant twice and insisted she have abortions both times. I shudder to think of the guilt over that. Olivia had several abortions, too. Her father had sex with her from the time she was little, but she repeatedly told us how *bad* she was for taking his car when she finally ran away from home. How our abusers have warped our perspectives!

Meg was pregnant when she married the father of her baby, who happened to be her dad's best friend. Just that statement was enough to give me the creeps. Her dad introduced them! He shared his only daughter with his buddy! Sick. She's twenty-three now, still married to a fifty-year-old. She went from her father's bed to a father-figure's bed. I think she's *still* submitting to incest, but she can't see it. She says he's different.

Susan huddled in a corner the whole time, and when she was asked to share, she fled into the hallway to cry. My heart went out to her. She's so beautiful, but she carries herself as if she doesn't deserve to be among the living.

It was especially painful to watch Annie speak of her earliest memory, when she was two years old. (I used to have a hard time believing anyone could remember back that far, but I've developed a whole new respect for the human mind. There's more under the surface than we're willing to acknowledge. Most of us have shut down access to ninety percent of our brains.)

Annie curled herself into a tight ball, her voice faltering as she struggled to describe the scene of abuse she had shared with me a few days ago. I knew what she was seeing, but the others saw only her fear.

She faded away from us. Even in her silence, I felt her terror as the memory swept over her, and she was back there again. The longer she was silent, the more desperately I wanted to take her hand and pull her from the whirlpool of shame into which she was disappearing.

Finally I couldn't stand any more. "Annie," I said quietly, from where I sat across the room.

Annie's eyes slowly focused on me.

"Did you seduce your father when you were only two?"

Her body jerked back as if she'd been hit by a blast of arctic wind. But she was back with us, and verbal again.

"Well . . . no!" Her posture seemed to relax a little.

"It wasn't your fault, Annie," I said. "Your father was a sick, violent man, and you were a helpless little child. You were innocent."

The group focus shifted to me. Well, I guess I did take over, when I was trying not to. But everyone in the group was relieved to be pulled away from the pain of the flashback we'd all witnessed. Helen studied my face for a minute and then changed the subject to something less intense.

But I think *my* intensity is just getting rolling. When I think of the cumulative agony of the eight victims in that room, I could scream. But this feeling isn't the fear and shame and sadness I've been drowning in for months. It's anger. What right does any human being have to cause the pain I saw in those faces? They don't deserve the submission of our tears. What they deserve is retribution!

We victims take on the responsibility for the sin and shame of what happened, because our abusers won't acknowledge their real responsibility. We're so immersed in shame, we can't see how ludicrous it is to call the child the responsible one.

We were all stunned by Annie's display of shame for what happened to her as a toddler, before she could communicate in clear sentences or reach a doorknob or go to the bathroom by herself! What control did she have over any aspect of her environment?

It brought home to me how very monstrous are the lies they told us. How horrified society should be that an abuser could use a baby as he did and then brainwash her into believing that it was *her* badness that manipulated *him* into violating her innocence at that age! She was helpless!

And because of the emotional and spiritual abuse we suffered, we were just as helpless to defend ourselves at the age of five or nine or eighteen. We're *still* helpless, as long as we believe their lies about our responsibility. Until we stop accepting the shame they dumped on us, we can never get out of that whirlpool that sucks us ever deeper into despair.

We've been victims all our lives, and we're victims still. But I refuse to be counted a victim any longer. I survived it, and I will get beyond it, and I will not live with my abusers' shame anymore. Enough is enough. .

Friday, January 12, 2:00 A.M.

Oh, what I would give for a week's worth of sleeping eight hours straight each night! But sleep disturbances are common to survivors. And we have to learn to live with what we've got. So I write. *Do you have a message for me, Lord?*

I read my last journal entry to Jason in yesterday's session. When I finished, he said, "That sounds to me like a declaration of independence."

I gave him a wry smile. "Yeah. But a declaration of independence is just the beginning. The American declaration was followed by years of war!"

"What battles are going on right now?" he asked.

I paused to analyze. "I guess part of me is still afraid to be angry because it makes me like my family. Because God might not love me if I'm angry."

"Does God withdraw his love as easily as that?"

I thought about how differently I see God now. "No," I replied honestly. "I know God accepts me. But that little girl inside me still needs constant reassurance. Anger still scares her."

"Hasn't that little girl been angry all along?"

He had me there. "I guess I've already admitted that. I've tried to keep it bottled up inside. But it explodes when I lose control."

"Your family taught you by example that anger was 'bad.' While they were raging out of control, did you ever have permission to express anger?"

"No. My expression of anger would have been a trigger for more of their rage to be dumped on me."

Jason nodded. "But you've learned that you were not responsible for the dysfunction in their lives. Their behavior when they were angry was wrong, because it hurt other people." He pulled a Bible from the shelf behind him. Yet in Ephesians 4:26 we're told, 'In your anger do not sin' (NIV). It's a given that human beings do get angry.

"God himself has anger against those who harm His children," Jason went on, turning to another passage. Psalm 78:50 shows us that God premeditated the action His anger would create: 'He prepared a path for His anger' (NIV).

"Jesus was angry, but we know that He was without sin. So there must be a way to allow for anger—righteous anger at injustice—without sinning. In fact, there are times when anger is appropriate and necessary for our well-being."

So what I need to sort out now, as I write this, is what *is* appropriate anger?

God gave us the emotion of anger, as He gave us the whole range of human emotions. The purpose of anger is self-protection when wrong is done to us. It's a healthy defense response when we are hurt. In a functional family, there would have been universal outrage if I had been victimized as a child.

Healthy anger has been the catalyst for much good in the world. Without anger, would injustice ever be righted? We'd still have slavery and children working in sweat shops fourteen hours a day. But where exactly is the line between healthy expression of anger and sin in the effects I allow my anger to create?

That's not a simple question. I can take it to an extreme and know that it would be sinful to take a shotgun and go after the people who hurt me. But in the gray area, I know that if my anger does get out of hand and I commit sin, God desires to heal it, not to condemn it. He's going to love me, anyway.

I reread Ephesians 4 just now, and verse 31 jumped out at me: "Get rid of all bitterness, rage and anger, brawling and slander, along with every form of malice" (NIV). My family would probably say that verse matches their message: "Don't *be* angry! Anger is bad." So I've been afraid to face my natural anger.

I tried all my life not to be angry, because I didn't want to be like *them*. But the anger only went underground and then shot out like a geyser when I was under stress. God's way of getting "rid of all bitterness, rage and anger" wouldn't be "stuffing it;" it would be expressing it *without* hurting anyone, even myself.

God already knows about my anger. If I acknowledge it and release it, He won't love me less. Surely He would approve an honest admission of anger far more than the denial of reality—the *lie*—I've lived in all these years.

Yes, I am angry!

God, help me to rid myself of that poisonous bitterness that has seeped into every part of my life. It feels like a volcano ready to erupt from inside me. I don't know how to control it. Show me how to express it without damaging myself or others. Show me a safe path for my anger to follow. Help me to submit it to Your will.

Saturday, January 20, 10:30 P.M.

This afternoon I escaped from the family while David watched the kids, and went alone to a movie theater, hoping for respite from the insistent pressure of abuse issues that continue to boil inside me. Popcorn in hand, I settled down to the opening credits of *Driving Miss Daisy*, prepared to focus on enjoying the gentle story it was reported to be. It didn't quite work out that way.

There came a moment when Dan Aykroyd's character appeared in Miss Daisy's kitchen. As the camera drew back for a three-quarter shot of him from across the room, I stopped hearing the continuing dialogue. My mouth went dry and my heart began to pound with fear.

judy was abruptly transfixed in horror by Dan Aykroyd's belt buckle, just above the zipper fly in generously cut pleated-front dress pants. Dacron-and-wool blend perma-prest, with cuffs. *Richard's pants*, bought at J. C. Penney's, and the only kind he wore. They loomed above me on the giant screen, on the body of a man who resembled Richard in his sharp nose, sloping shoulders, and his soft, stocky build.

There was a physical likeness, and perhaps a similar way of moving. And the movie's story, wardrobe, and set design were all intended to produce the experience of the late fifties and early sixties—the time of my childhood. But *judy's* frightened gaze was centered on a middle-aged man's crotch.

It was a frozen instant in time that smothered me again in my old recurrent dread. It took at least twenty minutes for

141

me to talk myself down from it, to bring myself back to the present, reassuring *judy* that it wasn't Richard on the screen. That nothing bad was going to happen. That she was safe.

Can I have any lingering doubt that my fear of Richard was related to sexual abuse? I don't think so.

I am sick of the fear. I am tired of the shame. And I am sick and tired of looking for approval from people I cannot respect!

Wednesday, January 24, 11:45 P.M.

I can't sleep. But I'm finally seeing how much resistance I've had to allowing myself to be angry at Mom. Yes, she is a victim, and that is the source of the dysfunction that caused her to emotionally abandon me. She has lived with pain. Poor Mom.

I have lived with pain, too. That fact doesn't absolve me from responsibility for ways I have hurt my own daughters. I haven't even begun to address my dysfunctions in parenting. But my children do harbor anger against me for hurts I can't see yet. They haven't learned to express it, but when they are able to, I can't deny them the right to voice their rage. They're entitled.

Every human being in the world is the victim of sin and victimizes others to a greater or lesser degree. I'd be pretty codependent to say that every other victim in the family chain above me and below me deserves to express their anger, but I'll be the one who doesn't. I can't carry Mother's responsibility or anyone else's. All I can handle is my own.

I guess *judy* has needed to talk to Mom for a long time, but I haven't let her. She and I have both been afraid. But I'll give her a chance.

Mama, I feel so sad about what happened to me. I think I'm mad, too, but I'm scared to be mad at you because I need you to love me.

142

I never meant to be bad, but you always told me I was. You were always so unhappy and I thought it was all my fault. I never thought you loved me. Never. But I had to pretend that you did because that's what mothers do, isn't it? You were the only mother I had, and if you didn't love me, maybe you'd go away and I wouldn't have anybody. Even when you were there, I felt so alone. You never ever saw who I was.

Look at me! Have you ever seen me? Have you ever listened to me? No!

You can't hear me at all, can you? You can't hear me because you built a wall around yourself to protect you, but you left me outside the wall like a sack of garbage, with nobody to protect me from Gary or Hank or Dennis or Richard or anybody else that wanted to use me.

I was your human sacrifice! But you never even thought I was human, did you? Well, I was! I am! I deserved a mother, but you never were one. You set me up! You were too afraid of men to face them and protect me. You were so afraid they would hurt you that you offered me to them instead.

Don't tell me you never knew! I was screaming for help all my life, and you ignored me. They hurt me enough. But the worst was that you didn't care about me. You treated me as if I were worth nothing.

You never noticed they were using me—raping me—because every minute they spent with me was one less minute you'd be bothered with me and one less minute you were at risk from them. You raped me every time one of them did, by giving them permission with your silence. I hate you for that.

I tried so hard to love you for so long. I thought maybe you'd love me back. No. Well, there wasn't any reason to love you, anyway. So I take it all back and you can't have any of my love, either. Not that you'll notice. But that isn't because I'm bad, it's only because you're so blind.

I hate you for making my life such a nightmare and for always making me ashamed. You made me feel lower than anyone else in the world. And that didn't start the first time I got raped. It started when I was born.

I'm giving up needing you to be a real mother to me. You never could, anyway. I don't have a mother. Nothing new. I got through it without a mother all along, so I'll be my own mother now.

You've been in control of my head all my life! I want you out of there now! I don't want to hear your poisonous messages. I won't listen anymore.

Letting go of you is hard, Mom, but it isn't impossible. I'm responsible for myself now. I'm the only parent my inner child ever had. If I'm going to protect her, I have to help her see the truth of how much of her pain came from you. I won't expose her to you anymore. I choose to honor her strength in surviving.

Healthy self-respect ("love your neighbor as yourself" assumes we *do* love ourselves) demands that I keep myself safe from abusive relationships. So I'm withdrawing, Mom. Maybe someday, if you're willing to face your own pain and your own responsibility, you can convince me it might be safe to begin a new relationship with you.

Saturday, January 27, 3:00 P.M.

Having opened up a door to allow my anger out, I shouldn't be too surprised to find myself seething with it. I've been venting some of the pressure by running more—six times in the last couple of weeks. I managed a whole mile just now without stopping to walk. I'm pushing myself the way I want to push *them*.

My husband offered to borrow some boxing gloves so I could discharge some of this furious energy by pummeling him or some inanimate object as a scapegoat. But I'm not comfortable with that.

When I run (although my pace should more properly be called a jog), it's easy to visualize the shaming, sneering faces of my abusers. My mother stands ahead of me, planted flat-footed, her hands on her hips and her face a mask of rage. "Don't you *dare* look at me that way, young lady!" she hisses. And I put out my hands and push right through her. She doesn't control me.

Gary looms up now, a nasty smirk on his face. "You think you're so smart, huh?" I can hear his chuckle, rising in pitch to a silly, nervous giggle. How pathetic he is! He evaporates as I pass through him.

Then there is Richard, shaking his finger in my face, his blue eyes drilling right through me, invading me. But he's only a mental image. He disintegrates as I continue on.

Together they call after me the combined messages of my childhood: "Why bother trying? You *can't* . . . you're too bad, stupid, ugly, fat, clumsy, lazy!" Those lies have all been invalidated by the fact that I survived them.

God values me! He gave me the strength to cope with the pain they inflicted and the courage to face the shame and get beyond it. I have passed by the limitations they have imposed on me all my life.

I'm getting healthy while they're still frantically paddling to keep their heads above the cesspool of their shame. In their own frightened efforts to stay afloat, each pushes the others under the surface. They're only trying to survive, even if it means drowning an innocent child in the slime. It's just never occurred to them to look for a ladder to climb out of the cesspool. That ladder requires facing themselves. They're afraid to consider such a solution.

But I'm *out* now. If I'm going to be the person God designed me to be, I must stop allowing their old messages playing in my head to control me. My running, like my recovery, goes against every one of the expectations of worthlessness imposed on me by them. But there's another way they've still kept me a victim to them.

Every time I compulsively eat what is not healthy for me, one of *them* is in my head holding the spoon, saying, "Go ahead, you're hopeless anyway! Even if you deny yourself this, you've never succeeded at anything, so what makes you think you'll continue on a diet and reach a goal? Eat, *eat!* It'll keep you from *feeling* the fear and the self-loathing we taught you all your life. It'll keep you numb and passive and *available* for us to control. It'll keep you heavy and awkward and hopeless. Go ahead, eat. It'll make you the person we want you to be. *Ours!*"

My addiction to sugar is in response to those messages. I haven't slit my wrists, but I've been slowly self-destructing, stuffing myself with a poison that blocks my energy and will and self-confidence. It's self-destructive to keep myself a victim just because they wanted me to be a victim. But I won't let them have me anymore. They've been in control too long and I'm taking the reins away from them. I will be who I decide I am, not what they tell me to be. My body is mine at last, the temple of the Holy Spirit, instead of a hiding place for all the ghosts of my past. I'm evicting them.

Thursday, February 1, 4:00 P.M.

I got back from running a few minutes ago. I'm going a mile four days a week now, and it feels good. I can feel my muscles working. I can feel my lungs laboring to process all the free air I'm taking in. It's hard work, but I'm quite capable of handling hard work. My numbness is beginning to wear off, and I'm developing a whole lot of respect for this body I dissociated from so long ago. But . . .

As I walked a half-mile to cool down after the run, another memory popped to the surface. It's been there all along, but it's as if I just didn't look in the right direction for it.

146

I remembered standing in my mother's bedroom, in the dimness of late afternoon. No one else was at home. I walked resolutely to her dresser and opened the top right-hand drawer.

Reaching directly into the back right-hand corner of the drawer, behind the underwear, my hand closed around a plastic case. I drew it out and opened it. Inside was something familiar, yet strange. I studied it in confusion and fear. It was a flexible wire ring, about three inches across, with a latex covering that stretched across it to create a shallow concave shield. It was my mother's diaphragm.

Remembering it this afternoon, I stopped walking and stood still on the sidewalk of my street. The memory ended, but my brain continued on: *Did Richard use my mother's diaphragm on . . . in me?* I don't believe the question would be in my head unless the answer is yes. No one makes up such a revolting idea.

This memory raises an issue I've avoided looking at. For Richard to use birth control with me, I must have been at least thirteen, when I had my first period. And if he was having intercourse with me then, there would have been nothing to stop his continuing until I left home at eighteen. *Oh, God.*

Now as I write, I'm looking for the memory that corresponds to this one. The memory of when it happened.

I remember one of my younger brothers once telling me he had observed Mom and Richard having sex. Why, then, do I have a picture in my head of . . . not my brother telling me the story . . . but of my own observation from the doorway—Richard's white skin, bare haunches between the legs of a still form under his weight? Was it Mother? Why would I question that? He was married to Mother and still is.

I couldn't have my brother's visual memory inside *my* head. But Mom and Richard would have locked the door.

And the fear I had of Richard was so strong I would never have imagined trying to sneak a peek at them, as my brother had done. Where did this come from? I can't explain it.

I *am* feeling a difference from the last major flashback I had. Yes, I'm in the middle of anxiety over this. I'm feeling grief and sadness and anger over this. What's missing is *shame*. For the first time, shame is *not* part of this memory. It belongs to someone else. Perhaps my inner child believes at last that she is not at fault. Isn't it about time?

Friday, February 2, 7:30 A.M.

I woke at 1:45 this morning with the memory I've been searching for in my head. Actually, it's not much clearer than what I wrote yesterday. But I *know*.

Standing at the doorway of my mother's room, looking toward the foot of the bed, I watched Richard's naked body moving rhythmically. I can see the legs spread beneath him, but I can't see her face. Because it's *me*.

I said once before that I didn't have any memory of having observed from the ceiling what was happening to the little girl on the bed, as so many survivors have experienced. But this memory is my version of dissociation. Usually I just daydreamed—went somewhere else inside my head—so I didn't have to feel what I couldn't prevent. But this time, part of me left the body on the bed and watched from the safety of the door.

So, Richard raped me, too. With my mother's diaphragm, so he could take a perverted pleasure in shaming the mother and the daughter at the same time! Of course I was afraid of him. I was helpless to stop him.

It's interesting that I acknowledged that flashback at 1:45, turned over, and went back to sleep within a half-hour.

Saturday, Februaty 3, 9:30 A.M.

Last night the volcano erupted. The anger my inner child always carried for all the wrongs done to her exploded outward.

But first I grieved. David had picked up hamburgers on the way home from work, and the girls ate in front of the television while David and I talked in the bedroom. I dumped the memory of Richard raping me with Mom's diaphragm. And he silently held me while I cried.

I sobbed for over an hour, letting my inner child cry out all the why's that couldn't be answered. She never had a chance to say no. She never screamed out loud or struggled or kicked them or beat upon their chests. She never told what they did to her. But it was never less than rape. She was helpless.

They stole all her power of resistance and shamed her for being such a victim to so many. They mocked her for the pleasure response she couldn't help having, and they denied her any help to understand any of it. They left her to figure it out all alone. Alone. She was only a child! But she was never allowed her innocence.

When the tears finally slowed, David and I took a walk. He let me talk it out, and my grief receded as fury took its place. I wanted to take a baseball bat to each of the people who had hurt me. I wanted to smash them the way they had smashed me, leaving me groveling for crumbs of affection none of them were willing to give.

The walk did not expend my furious energy. We arrived back home with me still shaking with rage and needing some physical expression to rid myself of the poisonous bile that rose in my throat.

I retreated alone to the bedroom while David took the girls to the store. With no one home to hear me, I raged at them all—my mother, Gary, Richard, Hank, and Dennis. I threw pillows around the room. I screamed until I was hoarse the accumulated bitterness of the injustices I had suffered. I cursed them for the crimes I could enumerate and for all the buried rapes I may never consciously remember.

By the time David and the kids returned, my volume was reduced to muttering, but my anger was still white-hot. I kissed the girls good night, then gathered up four three-inch phone books and a wastebasket and withdrew to the bedroom again.

While David put the kids to bed, I spent an hour's worth of the adrenaline that accompanied my anger to fuel the violent destruction of those phone books. Every muscle in my body participated in the wrenching mutilation of thousands of pages.

In the energy I expended, I forcibly expelled the hatred I had harbored for thirty years of painful silence. I named each of the hundreds of injuries they had caused me, in damage to my self-esteem and sexuality and ability to function in society as a normal human being. I ripped apart the lies that bound me to their cruelty.

By the time the books were reduced to drifts of shredded newsprint on the carpet, my hands and arms ached pleasantly, all the way to my shoulders. I gathered the mess into the wastebasket and carried it to the fireplace in the living room, where a low fire was burning as David sat alone watching television.

Then, in silence I fed handfuls of paper into the flames. I watched for a long time as each of those bits smoked and curled and flashed into furious flame for such a brief moment before their heat cooled. Finally the last of the blackened edges glowed and went out, leaving gray ash that will disintegrate into fine powder when I sweep it all into a dustpan and throw it out.

That's how much their lives mean now. That's how powerful they are in my life—just gray ash that crumbles at a touch. Their illusions of power are only fragile façades to protect their own fears.

I will always hate the sins they committed against me. But they don't have any more hold on my life. God help them. I will not live my life for them anymore.

CHAPTER 10

Rock Throwing

In the midst of venting old rage, confronting my family with their sins was appealing. It wasn't until a full year later that I recognized my heady feeling of power at the time had been merely an illusion of healthy self-control. My old fear still lurked just beneath the surface.

Psychology says anger and fear bring on our "fight or flight" responses. Our brains reflexively route the greatest blood flow to our muscles, readying us for a physical response to danger. Which leaves our thought processes at their very weakest. Logic deserts us. So in anger, we're at our worst in a confrontation.

judy was still only nine years old. I doubt that I would have had the inner strength to stand up to my family's denial without relapsing into shame. The sight of me quaking with fear would have been a flashback to every time they controlled me with blame. Far from convicting them, I believe it more likely would have entrenched them in their self-righteousness.

Thursday, February 8, 2:00 A.M.

Tuesday night in our group session, the others were startled by my obvious anger.

In the past two sessions, Susan has finally relaxed enough to share a little bit. This time she told us how her sixteen-year-old brother had crept into her bed when she was eight. She insisted it only happened once and that she wants to get past it and love him now, because he doesn't have much time left. He's dying of AIDS.

"Good!" judy blurted out. Instantly I regretted saying it. What kind of bloodthirsty person will they think I am? How about some humanity, some Christianity here? Seeing the shocked looks on every face except the therapist's, I went into a sudden panic attack. For the rest of the session, I silently shamed myself without mercy for saying such a vile thing. I've unleashed a monster inside myself!

But maybe that's a fairly accurate statement of how victims really feel about their abusers, if we can ever get beneath all the denial and defenses we put up. I was taught to express only a narrow range of "acceptable" emotions in my family. "Only vanilla", as Jason put it. No other flavors allowed. Under the surface boiled a bitter concoction of the hatred that was a natural response to my pain. However shocked I am to discover that fury now, I'm finally honest enough to acknowledge that it existed all along. Doesn't God understand that about me?

No one was ever angry on my behalf—in protection of me. But isn't God angry at the crimes committed against me? Matthew 18:6 sums up His protectiveness of me as His child:

"But if anyone causes one of these little ones who believe in me to sin, it would be better for him to have a large millstone hung around his neck and to be drowned in the depths of the sea" (NIV).

But society turns away and coughs delicately, afraid to get involved in "family" matters. The women's movement has raised a lot of ire in defense of women who are the victims of rape. Yet when the newspapers report child sexual abuse, we still hear that the child was "fondled," "molested," "touched inappropriately." Let's call it what it is! Whether or not a penis ever enters a vagina, the child is raped—sexually and emotionally violated! And she has no adult coping skills to deal with rape.

Even *rape* is too kind a word. The most *honest* words to describe the way we were used are words Christians aren't supposed to say. Maybe the four-letter variety are the most appropriate descriptions for what really happened. The same vocabulary used for healthy married sexuality sanctioned by God is surely not applicable for child sexual abuse!

Intercourse is a word that implies mutuality between two people, not the relationship between a victim and a rapist. My abusers were not making love to me! They never *fondled* me. They used my body like a piece of meat, without any concern for the fact that they were ravaging my spirit and mind.

I've never drawn a breath my entire life that was not polluted by the effects of their warped attention. They didn't just rape my body over and over again. They raped my mind. They skewed the framework of my thought processes. My confused understanding of the foundations of human relationships is manifested in a thousand details of my life. As my friend Annie said, "Every characteristic of my personality displays my history." What enormous losses we have!

155

Friday, February 16, 2:30 A.M.

Olivia and two other group members have quit coming to the sessions. Apparently the intensity was more than they could deal with right now. Funny, I can't find a way to take a break from *my* painful healing process. I wonder if they'll ever finish theirs.

Therapy *is* a devastating experience. There have been times I've wanted to quit, too. But the old feelings block my view of anything else right now. As frightened and exhausted as I have been in the midst of this pain, I know I can't abandon my inner child's need for healing because my adult self is afraid.

There is a cancer in *judy's* soul. As the only parent *judy* has, I would be abusing her further if I told her, in effect, "Go back to playing your games, honey. You're not really sick, anyway. I won't let those mean old doctors cut you open to take out that little bit of tumor." No. The most loving thing a parent can do is to face the fears—her own and her child's fears—with that child, and walk together through the pain, so she can be cured of the cancer. So I've kept on, one foot in front of the other, often hesitating, always apprehensive.

One step at a time has brought me to this group, thinking I needed a group desperately. I'm appreciating the sense of community we're developing, but I'm surprised to find that the most important lesson I'm getting here is a confirmation of what I've already accomplished. I guess I've come a long way to be here.

Meanwhile, on Tuesday night, we were down to five group members. Consuela was struggling with the need to document her abuse so they can have specific dates and events to convict her father. The prosecuting attorney asked her to try to find more memories. She didn't like the idea and didn't want to look for more stuff. She didn't know how to go about searching, anyway. I suggested drawing a diagram of the house. It sure brought up some of my details for me!

How many of us have sufficient *evidence* to legally convict our abusers? Only a tiny percentage. The court system doesn't have any space for memory repression. But how else could we have coped when there was nobody who cared enough to help us acknowledge that it happened?

Every day, in the midst of the panic and the aloneness, I must have told myself over and over, "Don't think about it. Pretend it didn't happen. Don't let anybody *know!*" Eventually I got enough practice pushing it out of my thoughts that the topic didn't come up anymore. I had lost conscious access to the memories that would have convicted them in a legal confrontation.

Meg confronted her father last week. She told how painful that discussion had been; that she had broken into tears several times. His response was not what she had hoped for. He did acknowledge having sex with her. But he said it wasn't abuse, because he wasn't hurting her. She liked it. As simple as that. *Liar*.

She told him she didn't want a relationship with him at all from now on and that she would protect her children from him. He stayed firmly in denial even after she told him how difficult her therapy has been, the effects it has had on her life. But whatever his response, she said she was glad she had gone through it because she felt as if she were in control of her life again and not a victim anymore. She feels powerful.

That's a feeling I'd like to have. Since I started therapy, I haven't thought I wanted to confront my family because I was afraid I'd get sucked into their craziness again and I'd end up doubting my own perceptions. But fear of that has taken a backseat now to the fact that I want to tell them very clearly that my daughters will not be available for a relationship with them. I will not risk their innocence just to fulfill family expectations.

Of course, Hank is dead, so he can't hurt anyone anymore. I don't expect *ever* to want any alliance with Richard or Gary. I'd be abusing myself to seek people who don't have any nurturance to give. All they can offer is poison. They've had a lifetime of practice in shifting blame from their own shoulders. And statistics give scant hope of chronic child sexual abusers willingly going through counseling and staying away from other children. I wonder if Richard and Gary are molesting little girls now?

Then what would I hope to achieve, other than keeping my daughters away from them? Well, someday I'd like to have a relationship with my mother. I can hope that confrontation would cause her to face her own responsibility and get help for her old wounds. I want her to experience God's love and healing.

Besides, there's a strong consensus among the authors of recovery books that confrontation is the step that disconnects us from the abusive past. So we can take back our power and be in control of our lives again. Control! I've never had that in my whole life!

I don't want to keep avoiding my family forever without explanation. I don't want to live in fear that they'll show up on my doorstep, suitcases in hand, with no warning, and force a confrontation by their timing and not my own. I *do* want them to know the effects of their actions on me. I'm tired of the secrets and I'm tired of protecting them.

Jason was cautious about my new theme of confrontation when I saw him yesterday afternoon. He raised some questions about potential hurts I might suffer by their response. And he wondered how real is the possibility of my mother's healing as a result of my confrontation. I'll do some exploration along those lines and I won't rush a final decision. But it *is* my decision to make, not Jason's.

At the end of my session, without comment, he handed me a book and a tape to take home—*Forgiving our Parents,* by Dwight Lee Wolter, and *Forgive and Forget,* by Louis Smedes. It wasn't till I settled into a chair after running two miles and took time to look them over, that it dawned on me this was the first time he had brought up the topic of forgiveness, except for the instances of specific forgiveness aimed at particular actions during memory healing.

Forgiveness for *all* of them? For *all* the hurt? Is that what Jason has in mind? This is quite a departure from his consistent implication that it isn't time yet. Forgiveness!

I used to be eager to forgive. But now I find my inner child resisting. I'll do the assignments anyway, because I *always* do the assignments. Just like in school.

Monday, February 19, 4:30 P.M.

Last night something very disturbing happened. About 2:00 A.M., from the midst of deep sleep, I became conscious of being sexually aroused. I kept hanging on to sleep, fighting off the awareness of stimulation, thinking, *Oh, David, leave me alone. Can't you see I'm asleep? It isn't worth it.* Eventually the feeling faded and I sank back into slumber.

But then it started again. Stroking down my back, along my hip, and then between my thighs. Reaching between my legs, from behind me. Finally I shifted to accept the pressure. The feeling was strong enough to make me willing to enter into the pleasure, to waken for it. I swam slowly up, up to the surface of consciousness from the murky underwater depths of sleep.

In transition to wakefulness, I gradually took in the childlike security in the sensations of my arms wrapped tightly around Bear's fuzzy bulk, clutched to my chest as I lay on my side. I felt David's body curled behind mine, spoon-fashion, his knees fitted into the bend of my own knees. His breathing was slow and regular. His hand was still, and it was on top of the blankets.

Incest! My eyes went wide as I was suddenly awake and recognized that the source of my arousal had nothing to do with David. He hadn't touched me. I didn't know who had stimulated those feelings, but it felt like incest.

Horrified, I threw back the blankets and stood up beside the bed, shivering, clasping Bear against me. I breathed deep and willed my heartbeat to slow its sudden surge in pace. And I silently reassured *judy* that it wasn't her fault.

David never stirred. Finally I went to the closet for a robe and an afghan. I settled in the recliner with Bear, who was somehow *judy* again. I comforted her and told her I would never again let her be a victim to sexual advances she didn't want. Knowing she was safe, we slept at last, spending the rest of the night in the chair.

I had acknowledged my own pleasure, and by moving away from the "scene of the crime," I had said no to whoever initiated the feelings in my dream. Saying no was quite a satisfaction!

Just because I was aroused does *not* mean I started it. I was *not* responsible for an automatic physical reaction. It does not matter whatever they might have said in order to put responsibility on me. My nervous system was wired to be aroused as a reflex to that kind of touch. And I *won't* take the blame anymore.

Wednesday, February 21, 2:00 A.M.

2:00 A.M. The hour means something new to me now.

I read the last journal entry to Jason in our session yesterday afternoon. He surprised me with his response. "I wonder if you might interpret that experience as evidence that you were assaulted in the middle of the night?"

Instantly I shot back, "But Carla was in the twin bed next to mine!"

"Was there anything she could have done to stop it?"

I seized on a thought that would have meant it couldn't be true. "Wait! If it was Gary, she might have! She wasn't afraid of Gary. But . . ." I shook my head, discarding the idea. "If it was Richard, she couldn't have stood up to him. And it was Richard."

Jason nodded. "Sleeping through it was the safest thing she could have done. She had no power to protect you or herself."

A light bulb went on in my head. *"That's* the reason she's so protective of Richard! She must have survivor guilt, because she couldn't protect me. She was a witness to some of my abuse, and she repressed the memory so she wouldn't have to live with the fact that she 'let me down' by not stopping it. Her inner child still protects Richard, because if Richard is exposed as a child molester, then that little girl inside her will be exposed, too. She sees herself as an accessory to the crimes, as *bad* Carla!"

"So her denial is an effort to protect herself from her own shame . . ."

"Just like mine has been most of my life," I finished.

I'm sure Jason was right. I accepted the idea so easily because his suggestion of middle-of-the-night abuse struck a resonant chord within me. Part of me wants to deny it happened, but deep down, I know it's true.

Tonight, waking up at 2:00 A.M., right on the "schedule" I've developed during this year in therapy, confirms everything we talked about in that session.

At least three nights a week during this year (often *every* night), I have awakened for no apparent reason at about the same time—1:30 to 3:00 A.M. Yes, it has been an opportunity to listen to what God has to say to me. God works in all things for my good. But the underlying basis for my waking was that it was the time I was assaulted in my sleep.

It clears up some questions I didn't even know were there. When we were first married, David was amazed that I usually slept on my stomach. "How do you do that?" he exclaimed. "Doesn't it hurt your back?" But sleeping on my stomach was the most self-protective position I could assume. Even then, it left my backside exposed. Richard could rouse me from behind, like in my dream (which of course was a body memory).

Short of a suit of armor, there wasn't any way to keep from being touched that way in my sleep, even though I *never wanted it!*

This also answers why I've been so furious all my life at being awakened when I wasn't ready. I've never felt as though I was allowed to sleep as much as I wanted.

judy has always been angry at being awakened by the screams in the night that were the sounds of Mom and Richard fighting, and then at having her innocence stolen from her when she was least able to protect herself. She never released any of her own screams.

Richard always went to bed at 8:00 P.M. It was a way he got away from Mom, who stayed up until midnight every night. He could justify it by the fact that he got up to get ready for work about 3:00 A.M. But Mom never noticed his absence even earlier in the morning. He could wake up while Mom was in her deepest tranquilizer-induced unconsciousness and come to my bed. Then he woke her to cook his breakfast. Were the fights on mornings he hadn't released his frustrations through raping me? Or maybe they were after a rape—when he needed to shift the focus from his shame by picking a fight.

So that was the condition of their marriage—a holy estate? They're still locked together in mutual misery. God help them.

Saturday, February 24, 11:00 P.M.

I phoned Carla this morning. I didn't share any of my new memories with her. But she didn't like hearing that I was considering confronting Mom and Richard. I won't bother with Gary. The only contact he has with anyone in the family is an annual call to Mom, to "borrow" money from her. She still bails him out, incurring Richard's wrath.

I have to be realistic about Carla. She's on the fence now, but she'd rather not hear any of my stuff. Maybe she'll jump off the fence to protect Mom and Richard from my "persecution," especially since she hasn't accepted the fact that Richard abused me. Maybe I won't have a sister anymore.

For most of our childhood, we were enemies. That never changed until Gary left home. I thought we had become friends then, with that closeness continuing into adulthood. But now it looks more like codependency. Have her feelings for me always been based on my performance in supporting her? She doesn't answer back very often.

She told me how her life has fallen in on her. She's in despair over their financial losses. Every catastrophe that could possibly happen in her family has exploded in the weeks since Christmas. She is suffering. It looks like God has answered my prayer for her to *feel* her pain. Here's her invitation to change, to be healed. Getting to the bottom, perhaps she'll look up.

I asked her, "Do you hear a voice in all of this?" She evaded the question, but I was bold enough to press. "Isn't it all connected to our inability to be self-protective, to make healthy decisions, and to know how to love ourselves, let alone anyone else?"

"We both know our background has a lot to do with the mess our lives have been," she answered. There was a long pause. I just deal with it differently . . . or . . . not at all." Then she quoted her trademark philosophy: "Life is hard, and then you die."

My eyes welled with tears. If I could only make her recovery happen for her! "Life doesn't have to be like that," I said. "Mine isn't anymore." But she still can't trust life not to hurt her. She's stuck where she is. And she has resisted the idea of counseling each of the many times I've mentioned it.

I don't want to say good-bye to the loving sister image. But I finally have to acknowledge that in every conversation I have had with Carla, she has avoided hearing my pain because she's avoiding her own pain. She learned the family lessons well. She can't do any differently. I have to give up my expectations. Okay, so face the fact that that relationship is mostly illusion, too. I created it because I needed a family.

I told her that the next phone call would be up to her. I'm not going to pressure her about where she stands. She doesn't *have* to be on my side, if she doesn't want to. I'm giving her space to make her own decision, whether or not I confront them.

I guess I've never dealt with my feelings of loss about Carla. *judy*, do you want to talk to her?

I just wanted you to love me, Carla. Couldn't you tell Mom I didn't get any birthday cake? Couldn't you want to spend time with me instead of Gary? Couldn't you beat on Richard's back when he was on top of me in the middle of the night? Couldn't you make it stop? Couldn't you be my big sister? Couldn't you love me?

I wanted to talk to you about how lonely I was. I wanted to be able to share my hurt and hear what was hurting you. I wanted us to be able to cry together. I wanted you to believe in me. But you always sided with them, against me. I was the one who didn't fit in. I couldn't help being different.

You used to drag me out of bed on Saturdays to clean our room. What made it "our room" when it had no door to keep anybody out or any possession safe or private? If I cared about anything at all, it would be used as a weapon against me, to shame me. It was better not to feel, not to care about anything.

So why would I want to bother waking up to clean what didn't matter? I'd rather sleep or read or not exist. Richard had probably been in my bed the night before, anyway. Gary would be after me next, and I didn't have the energy. Let me sleep! I never got to sleep. But you made me feel guilty and lazy if I didn't help. You thought I was bad. Like everybody else.

So here I am in recovery, standing all alone with a very cold wind whistling around me. You are on your own, Judy. Just you and God. There are no background relationships.

Thursday, February 27, 7:30 P.M.

This afternoon, after I read the last entry to him, Jason pronounced me very healthy!

"Why?" I demanded. "Because I let go of the last shred of family?"

"Because you are facing reality about their capacities to be the family you want."

Sudden sadness threatened to crush my chest. "I still hope Carla will get help and face the truth. That I'll have her back someday. And Mom, too." I took a painful breath. "But I'm not basing my life on the possibility. I guess it's only hope for their healing. Not faith in it."

"They'll have to find their own faith in their healing," Jason answered. "What do you think it will take for them to recognize the truth about themselves? A year ago, could you hear the truth about yourself?"

"I heard *you*," I answered slowly. "I never heard it before."

"What made the difference?"

165

I had to think about that. Why could I face it now when I had always avoided self-examination before? "I guess it was trust," I said finally. "And knowing you accepted me. I willingly brought all that ugly stuff out to show you, because it was safe. You never labeled me. You never told me what was wrong with me, even though you saw it all along."

"How is that different from confrontation?"

Was that a thunderclap I heard? In an instant, I saw the "loving" church discipline I'd observed over the years—confrontations that turned into angry accusations and ferocious denials. I thought of Meg's confrontation with her father. She took back her power, in righteous indignation, but he never budged from his defensive position. He couldn't hear the truth. I thought of the fact that less than five percent of abusers ever admit any wrongdoing. I didn't expect anything different from Richard. And Mom—she's an abuser too, in her own way. Would my confrontation bring her healing or more denial?

And I thought of Carla. For months, haven't I confronted her with what I believe to be her need for help to heal her old wounds? She's still dodging the issue. She's still not willing to face the truth.

How is confrontation different from the trust Jason fostered so that I could face my own truth?

I answered at last, "Confrontation would have been your presenting me with a list of my sins as you saw them. My healing is a result of my own confession of my sins, voluntarily. That only happened because I knew you would accept me, anyway."

Jason nodded. "But since you've been in touch with your buried anger, confrontation has looked pretty attractive to you."

"Peer pressure!" I blurted out, surprised at myself. "I've felt so different from the others in the therapy group. I'm the only one of us who's working with a *man* therapist. I'm the only one who's getting Christian counseling, and some of the viewpoints differ. And the group's agreed stand on confrontation, like the books, seems to be that it's a necessary step, to be freed from the past."

"Do you have to be like the others in your group?"

I could have cried. "No . . . I am called to be like Jesus. I'm not called to be like others I know, even other Christians."

"What do you think Jesus would have done?"

Uh-oh. "Well, He wasn't shy about confronting sin where He saw it. He called the Pharisees a brood of vipers. But . . . more often—the times where we see healing taking place and lives changing—I guess Jesus just accepted sinners. Loved them anyway. When they felt how miraculously, unconditionally, He loved them . . . was it . . . the Holy Spirit . . . convicting their hearts?"

Jason smiled. "That's the Holy Spirit's job, after all."

"But what about the times Jesus *did* confront sin?"

"Did Jesus know their hearts?"

"Oh. But *I* can't see into the hearts of the people who abused me." I gave a mock groan. "I also don't have the same self-assurance Jesus had in the face of their denial and anger. Come to think of it, taking back my power doesn't sound very Christlike. I am powerless. My power comes from God."

"Well, let's not go too far in the other direction," Jason answered quickly. "Confrontation has its place. Most survivors confront their abusers eventually. With the Lord's leading and his timing, it can be a good step to take. You may come to a place when it's right for you to confront them.

"But my concern is for *you*. I'd hate to know that your inner child was traumatized again, when she's just begun to experience freedom from their shame.

"As far as disconnecting from the past," he finished, "haven't you already experienced a little of that?"

"In memory healing!" I gasped. *How had I gotten so caught up in the group's focus that I could forget the weight lifted in memory healing?*

"What do you think was the source of the freedom you began to feel after memory healing?" Jason asked.

"Well, it was God who healed me..." Back to the topic I'd been evading lately. I met Jason's eyes. "It was the forgiveness, wasn't it? Forgiveness of Gary and Hank and Dennis and myself."

Jason nodded. "Have the confrontations you've observed provided real freedom from the past?"

Reluctantly, I shook my head. "Not like the change I've felt."

So I guess my next assignment is forgiveness. That's a tough one. *Okay, Lord, I'm working on it. I hear you.*

Wednesday, February 28, 2:30 A.M.

Is there ever going to come a time when it will be natural and automatic for me to seek *first* God's will instead of fighting to arrange events for myself? Finally I step back and say, "Oh, yeah, what was it God wanted here?"

Maybe what I've really wanted was to see them squirm and suffer just a little. I'd like *them* to be *my* victims for a while. *Just let me throw a few more rocks at them before I forgive them. Just let me get some revenge first.*

But however much they might be squirming on the inside, they wouldn't lay down their arms as easily as that. The battle has been in an uneasy cease-fire during my adult life, mostly because we live in another state. But confrontation, with my throwing rocks at them, would bring out their big guns. I don't suppose I'm a match for their fury. Nor would I want to be.

And of course, my wishful thinking looks for a dramatic awakening in them which would bring about their tearful repentance. In my imagination, they would beg my forgiveness and commit themselves in unswerving dedication to their own therapy and healing. They would then *be* the family I've longed for. Violins would play and roses would bloom. Disney would make a touching movie about the bonds of love between our generations.

That isn't going to happen. Give it up, Judy. Even if they choose the path to healing, it won't be a quick fix. So if that's your real reason, now is not the time for confrontation. Spend your energy to finish your own work. And the next step in finishing your own work, for your own healing, is forgiveness.

Forgiveness. This is not a word from my native language. Nobody in my family ever taught me by example what it meant. I have heard the word in reference to God, of course, but it doesn't match the God I experienced. I've come to know Him differently since then, though. I know now that He has forgiven me. And I'm learning to forgive myself, although I'm not very good at it yet.

Forgiving the people who hurt me is scary. I've finally learned to validate the pain of my inner child. I've felt *judy's* terror, her betrayal, her loneliness, her hatred. And now, asking myself to forgive feels like having to set aside all those emotions that never got heard at all before this year.

I've denied my feelings all my life. Those feelings are a part of *me*. I've welcomed them home at last. I'm accepting myself—fear, rage, and all—after all these years. How can I accept those emotions honestly and still make room for forgiveness? Especially when *I don't want to*?

On a rational level, I'm very clear on the need for forgiveness. It frees me from the bondage of living in the sordid past. It allows my own self-forgiveness and acceptance of God's forgiveness of me. It gives me peace. It doesn't even matter if my family ever knows they've been forgiven. And it doesn't mean I have to continue a relationship with them.

But my guts still want to hold back. It doesn't feel safe to forgive . . . maybe they'll hurt me again. I've never taken care of myself before, but now I can. I want *me* to be safe.

I also know that hashing it over inside my own head will never resolve it. I'll never feel safe *enough* to forgive them on my own. I'll never feel that they *deserve* my forgiveness.

Oh. Like *I* never deserved Christ's sacrifice and forgiveness, either. I guess I have to trust God to take care of my safety. Step out in faith to forgive them whether they're aware of it or not. Whether they hurt me again or not. Whether they'll ever love me or not.

It still isn't fair, is it? Did Jesus have this argument with God in Gethsemane? I can understand why He sweat blood. "But they don't deserve it, God! They won't notice what I've done, and they won't appreciate it. None of them has a clue how hard forgiveness is for me. What I'm giving up for them! They'll mock me and call me a fake! . . . nevertheless."

Jesus trusted me to accept His gift. He asks me to follow Him and His example, so His sacrifice for me will be worthwhile. He went through it for me.

He's going to provide me the strength to forgive them. He doesn't expect me to do it alone. He'll heal the feelings, if only I'm willing. *Okay, God, I submit. It's too hard for me to do without you. Help me forgive them.*

CHAPTER 11

Letting Go

Somehow there was peace enough to let go of my compulsion to seek revenge. The process of forgiving began the cycle of grief again, and it intensified as I found myself releasing my hold on my will to control the circumstances and relationships in my life.

I shed a great many tears. But my grieving was an unyielding drive to move beyond the suffering. While the pain was still fierce, the desperation of the previous months was dissipating. We reduced the counseling appointments from bi-weekly to once a week.

God led me to gradually unclench my determined grip on the past. Paradoxically, in submitting to God's will, he swept me into a new level of freedom. How many of us waste the tragedies in our lives, bitterly clinging to our misery!

From an Edna St. Vincent Millay poem: "Count them unclean, these tears that turn no mill." My tears were pure; none were wasted.

Monday, March 12, 11:30 P.M.

I can't get to sleep. Does it have anything to do with the fact that Consuela's father's trial began today? The whole group attended.

On a break, someone expressed concern at the amount of anger the prosecuting attorney displayed in her opening statement. I replied that society *needs* to be angry at abusers. Without anger, children will never be protected from violence. Quit being polite about rapists! The prosecutor was modeling an honest emotional reaction to a heinous crime. In so doing, she gave the jurors permission to feel their own anger at such injustice.

Will we see justice for Consuela's father? I'm more inclined to think that real justice for child sexual abusers is the private hell of their own construction, built of their own shame and rage.

I guess God can take care of the rest. He has more anger against those who hurt us than we could ever summon. The Bible, expecially the Psalms, is full of examples of God's wrath against oppressors, while He offers loving compassion to the persecuted.

Isn't letting go of the need for revenge, letting God handle justice, the essence of forgiveness? My forgiveness doesn't say, "It doesn't matter what you did, it's all okay now." Instead, the message is, "It matters very much how you hurt me. I never deserved such treatment . . . but I'm not going to bear the weight of that painful connection with you any more."

172

My bitterness kept a white-knuckled grip on the chains that bound them and their responsibility to me. I wasn't going to let them off the hook. I've finally realized how heavy it has been holding them dangling off that hook for so many years. I've put too much energy into keeping them on the hook. I've stayed stuck in this spot, watching to see that they didn't get away.

Now I can relax my grip, release the hooks, drop the chains, and know all the while that there's a bigger hook holding them to their real responsibility—to God. He can keep watch over them and exact whatever price is necessary. It isn't okay that they hurt me. But God will settle every score.

I just recognized how human forgiveness differs from God's forgiveness. I can let go of my insistence on being in control of their accountability. But only God can clear the slate and restore their hearts to their former innocence, as if their crimes never happened. Even then, God doesn't rescue them from the earthly consequences of sin. They still have to deal with the broken relationships. They still have to learn to be healthy. I can't help them learn it by making myself available for their old ways of relating to me.

I've made a commitment to forgive, but my anger isn't instantly gone. It does seem to be lessening, though. Last Thursday Jason and I talked about finding a way to see my abusers as victims themselves, in order to be able to forgive.

It's easy to see my mother in that light. Gary, of course, was a victim—of our parents and probably of sexual abuse from our Uncle Hank. Hank himself spent the first ten years of his life in an orphanage, before being adopted by a single, handicapped woman, unheard of in 1940. Nothing about his life was "normal," and at the very least, he was the victim of abandonment and neglect. There was probably much more abuse than that to make him the sex addict he was. I know very little about Dennis, but that doesn't seem important.

Actually, I can't find much anger left against Gary or Hank or Dennis. It's not a coincidence that those are the three we addressed in memory healing sessions. Healing didn't just take away my shame. The forgiveness I was able to give each of them was real. Those incidents, those *people* don't matter now.

Richard? I haven't written any exploration about him. He was thirty-five and a bachelor when he married Mom, who was twice divorced with four kids. But he had no tolerance for children. He insisted that he and Mom eat dinner separately from the kids. He didn't want to hear us.

Yet Richard had to be in control of every detail of our lives. Like the fact that we had to ask permission to turn the TV channel, even if he wasn't watching. His tyrannical need to be in charge led him to humiliate everyone around him, to make himself feel more important.

I remember one of our miserable "vacations," when we would drive interminably across the country, we kids cooped up in a camper to verbally abuse each other just the way we had been taught. This incident was after Gary and Carla left home, so I was at least sixteen. Stopping at a grocery store, Mom asked if we needed anything. The kids weren't invited to get out of the camper, of course.

I whispered to her that I needed tampons. But upon their return from the store, it was *Richard* who handed me the little brown bag through the window, cackling gleefully, "Here's your stoppers!" My two younger brothers laughed at my sudden crying jag. Nothing I said would shut them up.

I guess I know why my mother subjected me to him. But what kind of cruelty had Richard experienced to make him so sadistic?

When I started college, I was still asking permission to go out on a weekly date, with a midnight curfew. He had always made a big deal out of approving dates. He would delay giving a direct answer, so I had to ask in advance, then ask again as the deadline approached. Now I think that little manipulation was a subtle reminder of his "power" over my life, which extended to his ownership of my body. Jealous of my dates, *expecting* that I was sexual with them, he reinforced my subjugation.

The last straw was the time when I was getting ready to go out on a date with David. I was eighteen, and in my freshman year of college. I was wearing a cute new shorts outfit I had made myself. I had been proficient at sewing everything I wore since I was thirteen; it gave me some measure of control, over my wardrobe at least.

Richard, coming into the kitchen, spotted my attire. He gave a scornful laugh. "You're not going to wear *that!* That looks like something only a whore would wear!"

His words were like a bludgeon to the forehead—the culmination of all the years of crushing shame. For the first time, I stood up to him. "Yes, I am," I said evenly, and the defiance that blazed in my eyes took him by surprise. He slapped me, hard. It was the first time he had done that.

I gasped in shock, then, amazingly, drew back to return the blow. But he caught my wrist before I made contact with his face. I don't remember any words exchanged between us after that.

I went to my room and started packing. There was pitifully little that had any value to me—mostly my homemade clothes. Mom fluttered around, trying to smooth things over. I told her I was moving to Grandma's house. I had nowhere else to go.

"But you know that's just the way Richard is!" she wheedled.

I turned to stare at her in disbelief. "Just because he has seniority in being unreasonable doesn't make him right!" It would have been pointless to have brought up the sexual abuse, even if I hadn't repressed it. Or maybe I *did* know it at the time, but the guaranteed response from Mom would have been more painful than leaving it unsaid. I moved to Grandma's house that night.

Now that I've unearthed it all, I can feel that pain afresh. If I was wearing something only a whore would wear, then Richard was calling me a whore. I had never chosen to be that. I was only what he, along with the others, had made me.

What made Richard the cruel dictator he is? What makes any person seek out the weakest spot in another, to create the deepest wound? Finally having let myself experience the depth of the fury I held inside, I know Richard's inner child had to have been terribly hurt to produce so angry an adult.

Richard's father was a mean drunk who lived with us for about a year when Richard's mother was in a mental hospital. It's obvious that their home was shaming and abusive. Richard was a Mama's boy, enmeshed with his mother. Was incest there somewhere? Possibly.

His mother fit into the extreme end of the spectrum of characteristics of a victim. She was an angry woman, grossly obese, who had severe emotional problems. But thirty years ago psychology didn't know what to do with incest survivors.

Maybe some of what we know as flashbacks today were incorrectly viewed as psychotic episodes then. They used drugs to calm the hysteria, but they weren't too successful at stuffing the memories back underground. Maybe they would have committed *me* to a mental hospital with the "nervous breakdown" I've been working through, if my crisis had happened back then.

If his mother was a victim, chances are she would have married a victim or an abuser. Well, Richard's father was an abusive alcoholic. I always hated him. He was a nasty, repulsive man.

And thinking of Richard right now, I'm not angry. I'm sickened. I'm appalled. I mourn for the waste of human life and for the misery caused by the sin people inflict on each other. How long can we be angry when we recognize the chain of hurt that goes back for generations and generations?

I've verbally abused my children, passing on the anger from my parents' abuse of me. My parents were trained to hurt me because someone took perfect babies and transformed them into clones of their own confused selves. But I have not gone through this torturous process of therapy only to watch the cycle continue. Forgiveness will break the chain, but to start over with my children, where do I learn how to love?

Wednesday, March 21, 11:00 P.M.

The verdict for the trial came in today. Consuela's father was convicted on one count of incest, acquitted on the other. I could see the jury really believed in his guilt, but some technical difficulties raised "reasonable doubts." He'll be sentenced in about six weeks, almost certainly to jail time. But I can't find any part of me that rejoices in his being locked up. It's just another sad story.

Sad. Isn't that how the God of love must feel, watching His precious children destroy each other in pointless grasping for power? As Jesus lamented in Matthew 23:37: "Oh, Jerusalem, Jerusalem, you who kill the prophets and stone those sent to you, how often I have longed to gather your children together, as a hen gathers her chicks under her wings, but you were not willing" (NIV).

He wants to heal us and comfort us. But we won't let him. Of *course* God hates sin! It hurts him to watch the "strong" crush the spirits of the "weak."

Humanity is a mass of angry, pain-wracked people all out to defend their own interests, and in the process, inflicting

177

more pain on anybody in their paths. We interpret every other person's motives through the gray mist of our own suffering.

Of course we're defensive! Everybody's been out to *get* us all our lives. The world's not a safe place for babies to grow up in. When you're rejected from birth, why would you ever believe anybody else would consider your needs? So we look out for number one and attack the competition.

That paranoia extends to our expectations of God. We go through the compulsive motions of our lives ignoring God, trying to pretend He doesn't exist. We focus on what we think we can control. If it's brought to our attention that God is aware of what's going on, we revert to a fetal position in a corner, panicked at our expectation of judgment, which equals abuse.

How we grieve the Holy Spirit when we reject His offer of perfect acceptance and love. It's the love we've all been so desperate for all our lives . . . and we can't see the gift because of our defensive anticipation of more pain. We are starving just outside the door to a sumptuous banquet laid out just for *us*. We're afraid to risk opening the door. It's intolerable to consider being vulnerable enough to reach out to lift that latch, to enter His presence.

I understand why humans resist giving up their anger. Anger feels safe, as if we are "in control." When you let go of the rage, you've laid down your "weapons." You're back to being vulnerable. Like a helpless child. Weak.

But unless you become like little children, you cannot enter the kingdom of heaven. Little children are weak, and they come face to face with that fact over and over again every day. Can't reach the doorknob. Can't pour their own glass of milk without spilling. Can't tie their own shoes. They are dependent on the love of a parent to provide what they can't do for themselves.

But I had to depend on people who weren't there. They wouldn't pour the milk for me, then they shamed me for spilling it. "Look how stupid she is; she can't tie her own shoes. Look how little she is; she can't open the door on her own. Look how weak she is; we can rape her and she can't even say no. We can use this weak child to satisfy our own lusts. Her needs aren't important. Don't bother to ask for your needs to be met. It's a sign of weakness to admit you have needs."

So they taught me that *weak* equals *bad*. Weakness invites abuse. The only hope of defending yourself against abuse is never to be weak. Be strong and invincible and competent for every occasion. Dazzle them with your myriad abilities, and they'll never see that you're vulnerable underneath. Fancy footwork will keep them guessing. Never let them see you sweat. Never expose your soft spot.

But now I discover that perhaps the whole world might not be out to rape me. That there is a way to trust and let myself be weak and still be safe. My inner child can be a child. She doesn't have to be perfect and strong. She's still afraid, but I remind her that God is protecting us both. He knows how weak I am.

Tuesday, March 27, 2:15 A.M.

Yesterday in my session with Jason, I told him that in letting go of my anger, I find myself awash in that same old sadness again. So I asked him, "What's the difference between grief and self-pity?"

"That's a good question," he said. "Self-pity doesn't go anywhere. But grief is an active process you move through. It's hard work to get to a better place than where you are. You're grieving, working on a new piece of ground every day. Your wheels haven't stopped moving."

Waking up and writing is part of my grief work, I suppose. I'm reminded of the beatitude: "Blessed are those who mourn, for they will be comforted" (Matt. 5:4, NIV). I never understood that one before.

True mourning requires an awareness and acceptance of our emotional reaction to a loss. So many of us deny our pain and avoid mourning. We push the feelings under the surface and pretend we're fine. We don't grieve the loss and never reach any resolution. We never get the comfort, the healing God offers.

But recovery psychology agrees with Jesus: Blessed are those who can deal honestly with their feelings of sadness, for they will become healthy. Actually, blessed are those who can honestly accept *all* their feelings, for they will resolve them.

Blessed are the meek, for they seek not after taking back their personal power through confrontation, but leave power and vengeance to God. Laying down the weapon of my anger, I feel helpless again, drowning in sadness. Haven't I done grief already? I'm so tired of it.

Thursday, March 29, 9:00 P.M.

Today Jason brought up the business of memory healing again. He suggested I evaluate what old wounds are still painful that we need to resolve. It also signals the beginning of the end, I think. I know it's not final. I still have work to do. But I have the feeling that very soon we'll wrap up this phase of therapy and begin the detachment phase. I'm afraid to think about standing alone, without Jason's support. I don't want to be finished.

I ran a mental inventory of my condition right now. To begin with, my relationship scorecard doesn't look so good. There's hope (I tell myself firmly) in my marriage and in my relationships with my children. But there's so much distance there right now. David is exhausted by the demands of supporting me through this intense grieving process. He wants *his* needs to be addressed, but I still don't have much energy for his needs.

And my background is all blown away. Besides, so many of what I used to see as close friendships look more and more like pure codependency. I can't be with those people and get healthy. Caretaking them drains me, takes my attention away from dealing with my real responsibilities, and keeps them from developing their own strengths through their challenges. So I'm without those "friends."

With an inventory like that and facing letting go of Jason, too, I get that old familiar feeling of loneliness. What I *want* is a mother! I want someone who knows my story and understands and accepts me unconditionally for who I am, flaws and all. Wait. That's not a mother, that's a therapist! That's Jason.

But I *do* want a mother. I have a long list of losses, but I guess she heads the list. I'm not feeling any more anger at her. I understand her too well to sustain the old rage. And God must be changing my heart. *judy* and I wrote a poem to her:

MY MAMA

If my mama could be who she wanted to be,
She'd cradle my head in her lap.
She'd stroke my temples
And croon my name soft and low.
She'd listen as I poured out my heart.
She'd cry with me for all my hurt.
She'd be on my side.
She'd believe in me.
She'd hold me close
Till I felt safe . . .

Which would be a long, long time.
She'd lock the door
So nobody could come in
To hurt me anymore.
She'd rub my back:
Gentle, rhythmic palms sliding
Shoulder to waist,
Shoulder to waist.
Till my sobs were spent
And my breathing slowed
And I sighed and slept
Against her warmth.
And she wouldn't move.
She wouldn't pull away.
She'd be there still.

Mama couldn't be who she wanted to be.
Neither of us got what we wanted then.
But my wounds are healing.
I've been held, and loved, and listened to.
I've been believed.
And I'm going to be all right, Mama.

I forgive her all over again. Lord, help me to keep on forgiving her.

Wednesday, April 11, 2:00 A.M.

Back in the midst of grief, the old questions recycle with more strength than I expected. Why me? Why any of us? It isn't fair that children should suffer the terrors we survived. Why does God allow such evil to exist in the world? I believe in a sovereign God. I know He has the power to do anything He chooses to do. Why didn't He stop them? I guess those questions weren't as fully resolved as I thought.

I understand it on an intellectual level. God allows evil because He has given all of us free will. If He removed all evil actions and the suffering evil creates, humanity would be mere robots.

In the free choice I've been allowed, I sometimes take actions that cause someone else discomfort and even pain. To remove evil, my freedom to make choices would be removed, because some of my choices are evil. It would be impossible to draw a line between the infinite gradations of the grayness between "evil" black and "good" white.

The parable of the weeds in Matthew 13:24–30, helps. Jesus identifies the source of evil—the "weeds sown among the wheat. . . . An enemy did this," He said. He was talking about Satan. But He instructed the servants not to pull up the weeds.

"Because while you are pulling the weeds, you may root up the wheat with them. Let both grow together until the harvest" (NIV).

Only God knows the full extent of the harm that would be done to the "wheat"—His chosen ones—if the evil were to be pulled out now. We see through the narrow perspective of our own suffering, but God sees all of time as one moment. At the harvest He will deal with the weeds.

Like I said, I understand it intellectually. Translating that understanding to my inner child is far tougher. She is still afraid and alone and ashamed much of the time. I can still see her curled into a ball, cowering in a dark corner.

Her fear can't be explained to someone who hasn't felt it. But it's related to the emotion moviemakers capitalize on when they produce a horror movie. There's always a victim who finds herself powerless in the face of impending disaster. The slasher or the rabid dog or the alien monster is ominously closing in, to a rising musical score, intent on destroying the victim, who doesn't know *when* it's going to happen. Audiences know that kind of horror. But they can leave after two hours. We who grew up in that terror had no escape. We lived in a chronic emergency state all our lives. I still re-live it.

My inner child wants to believe God really knows her paralyzing fear and her loss. She *has* felt Jesus' compassion for her and His comfort. But I find doubts I didn't expect. Jesus was never raped, was He? Did He ever experience that absolute helplessness?

I do know that, even without the sexual abuse, Jesus voluntarily lived through that helplessness when they nailed him to a cross.

But even so, what is held up as the epitome of human suffering—Jesus' death on the cross—was all over in a matter of hours, while incest victims live with their horror for years. We didn't deserve it, either. Annie, at two, didn't earn the violence inflicted on her any more than Jesus earned His crucifixion, did she?

There's an old song that insists, "Jesus bore it all!" But did He? (I never recognized that this resistance existed inside me at all before.) *judy* is still holding back her complete trust because she isn't sure Jesus understands her pain. She *wants* to trust. And I think God is willing to hear my questions. Okay, God, what *is* the answer? How was Jesus' pain—His "ultimate" sacrifice—greater than that of a suffering child?

I seek the answer in my chain-index Bible.

From the prophecies—Psalm 69:9 (NKJV): "the reproaches of those who reproach You have fallen on me." Isaiah 53:3–6, 12 (NKJV): "He is despised and rejected by men . . . He has borne our griefs And carried our sorrows . . . He was wounded for our transgressions, He was bruised for our iniquities . . . And the Lord has laid on Him the iniquity of us all . . . He bore the sin of many."

In the New Testament—Galatians 3:13 (NKJV): "Christ has redeemed us from the curse of the law, having become a curse for us . . ." First Peter 2:24 (NKJV): "who Himself bore our sins in His own body . . ."

Wait a minute. The concepts *sin* and *suffering* are all mixed up here. Is the Bible using these words synonymously? I guess if I believe what I wrote a few days ago—that the reason God hates sin is because of the pain it causes His children—then maybe I need to look at my internal definition of sin.

I used to think that sin was all the *bad* things people did that made God angry at us. God was a punishing judge, just waiting to catch us in a fault so He could jump on us in a rage. Sounds like Richard.

How would I define sin now? Well, sin isn't only the acts of murder or theft, or adultery committed by people. It's far broader than that. More than morally corrupt actions, sin is the global misery caused by those actions. Sin is the affliction that plagues us all our lives. Sin is responsible for the agony and hopelessness in every victim's existence.

"The whole creation has been groaning as in the pains of childbirth right up to the present time" (Rom. 8:22, NIV). Even the rocks cry out in anguish for the suffering brought into the world as sin.

I think we're just beginning to understand some of those long-term consequences through the recovery movement. Family dysfunction is caused by sinful actions and the surrounding secrecy and shaming, which is also sin. I grew up crippled by the chain of the sin sickness in my family that began long ago.

So if sin isn't just a specific *act*, but the *disease* that infects us all to greater or lesser degrees, how would that affect the way I see that Jesus "bore our sins"? On the cross, he became "a curse for us." In other words, He *became* sin in order that we could be freed from sin. If He *became* my altered definition of sin, then Jesus' hours on the cross when He was forsaken by God were a whole new category of suffering.

185

He didn't just suffer the physical pain in His own bleeding flesh and agonized muscles; He *experienced* the torment of every sinful human being in carrying their sin and pain. He didn't just carry the actions, He carried the consequences. Unbound from our human limitation of time and space, He *felt* the misery and despair of every broken moment in each of the billions of sinful lives on earth from the beginning of time until the end.

Humanity's sinful state is what separates us from God. God's holiness cannot tolerate the presence of sin. So while Jesus was making the supreme sacrifice of bearing, all at once, the world's whole screaming, shuddering, stinking, suffocating load of sin, God abandoned Him. He turned His back. He rejected the evil stench that engulfed Jesus' perfect shoulders so that he could embrace all the rest of us who claimed the gift of His sacrifice and were released from the burden.

I think *judy* is beginning to feel that Jesus does understand her pain. Every time she was raped, Jesus *was* there, not to interfere with the evil free choice of her abusers, but to suffer the agony with her. He lived every tortured moment of my life, hurting right beside me. And all the time, He was planning for the day when He would lift me out of the darkness of that deep pit, to set my feet on the solid rock of freedom. He always knew the healing He had in store for me.

I am again amazed by the sudden insight that appears on the paper beneath my pencil. You do answer prayer, God. *Thanks for clarifying my confusion.*

I just heard His response! "You're welcome." God's answer is far more than the mechanical rote phrase we rattle off for the sake of perfunctory politeness.

The Lord said I was welcome! Welcomed into His presence, into His overwhelming love, into His family. I'm not a stepchild. I am first in His heart. What comfort I can receive because I do know how much I am loved, and how much

Jesus *does* understand! This comfort is His blessing in response to my deep mourning. "Blessed are those who mourn, for they shall be comforted."

Friday, April 20, 2:45 A.M.

Yesterday, Jason asked me, "Who were you in high school?" By now I know him well enough to recognize that this open-ended question, combined with some associated comments, were hints giving me permission to talk about possible sexual relationships as a teenager. He was referring to the fact that promiscuity is a common response to sexual abuse. In effect, he's asking me if I'm carrying any more shameful memories that need healing.

I can see how easily something like that could happen to victims—we never learned how to say no, and the only "affection" we ever experienced was sexual. I'm a little surprised that promiscuity *wasn't* my profile. I can't explain why.

But his questioning prompted a memory of another kind, of an incident at school. Jostling through the press of adolescent bodies in the chaotic rush between classes, I spotted another girl, one I barely knew, walking a little ahead of me. She brushed her hand repeatedly across the back of her mini-skirt, in a self-conscious protective gesture that sought to assess the damage to her dignity. There was a red stain on the white denim, announcing her humiliation to anyone with eyes to see.

I quickened my pace to position myself behind her, to shield her "accident" from public view. But she was moving fast, in a frantic rush to reach the nearest rest room. The crowd of students blocked my path, and I couldn't catch up with her. I lost sight of her as two boys intervened just ahead of me. But I was close enough to witness the boys' exchanged glances and to hear their stage whispers, mocking her shameful condition. Then they burst into hysterical laughter.

If I had had a knife at that moment, I think I would have committed a double murder! Looking back now, I can see that my rage at their amusement was a response to my own shame in identifying with the other girl's predicament.

judy wanted to scream, *"Don't snicker at me for having a body that creates that humiliating mess every month! I never gave my body permission to be female! I was betrayed by my own flesh!"* If there had ever been a way to stop *being* female, with all the indignities attending that gender, I would have done it. The power to be in control of my body's functions seemed to be in the hands of nature and the males who used me. It was never mine!

Writing that story brings with it another enormous rush of grief, that my inner child should be forced to hate herself so much. Am I going be weeping forever? *Is this crushing sadness serving a purpose, Lord? I'm so weary of it.*

Wednesday, April 25, 10:45 P.M.

God, I feel so scared and alone. I know you're there, but everybody else I thought I could talk to is farther and farther away. Pretty soon, Jason won't be there to listen, either.

Yes, I did ask you to show me my boundaries, Lord, and the increasing distance with some I called friends is a clear message to me. They weren't safe relationships. But what do I have to replace them? I need people in my life. I'm afraid of being alone!

The biggest gap will be finding a way to process my innermost struggles without Jason. When the day comes that I don't have a therapist anymore, who's going to accept me unconditionally? Who's going to listen to my feelings, without misunderstanding or being disappointed in me or thinking I'm bad? Who will give me confidence when I don't think I have the strength to go on?

My husband. Is it David, God? I know he's the one you've given me, and he loves me, but he and I are perfectly opposite personality types! He doesn't understand me. Can he grow into that role? That's hard to believe. We can be one flesh, but we can't be one spirit, can we? You don't expect that, do you?

David tries, but he gets frustrated and impatient listening to me. Hearing my verbal processing is a burden to him, so I try to spare him. If I were to depend on him to listen the way Jason has, I'm afraid it would strain the relationship unbearably. He's already worn out by my grief.

He wants me to be finished already. I don't know how long that will take. And I don't think I have to apologize that I'm not healed yet. I didn't ask to be a victim! It's the depth of the wound that determines the duration of the suffering. But David wants me to be "fixed," so we can establish some "normalcy" in our lives. He can't listen the way I need him to.

Jason only listens so completely because he's a counselor, and I *pay* him to hear all the garbage I dredge up. That doesn't mean he doesn't care, but it *is* his job. He'd be very codependent to have given me all the hours he's been with me if he wasn't financially compensated. He has a family to support.

Reality reminds me that my husband has a different assignment in his own work. He's not my counselor. But who *will* be my counselor?

Jason has filled a multi-faceted role as counselor. He has been a healthy father figure, a teacher, a coach, an advocate, and a friend. Most importantly he has been a model of Christ's love and acceptance.

Through him I've experienced for the first time that there exists a relationship wherein I can be completely honest, myself, without fear of rejection. During the course of my therapy, Jason has been a physical stand-in for God. Like a stuntman in a movie production, he has stepped into the role of counselor during difficult scenes that required a physical presence. I had to experience a safe *human* trust relationship in order to heal the damages from human relationships that abused my trust.

So if Jason is a stand-in in counseling, then who can replace Jason? Oh. Only God. When you take away the "stuntman," you bring in the real thing. God. I didn't connect this before. Counselor. It's one of the names for God.

The counselor role that will be vacated in a few months isn't one David can fill, and Jason can't fill it indefinitely. Eventually when you get healthy, you discover that the therapist you've learned to trust is only a temporary substitute for the real relationship with God that will replace therapy. Even the best therapist is only a poor substitute for the counseling God can offer.

Every facet of the counselor role Jason has played—father figure, teacher, coach, advocate, and friend—are all ways God relates to me already. I have the *original* Comforter, not just a human shadow.

How can I *not* trust God to fulfill my counseling needs, when I've seen what amazing insights He has given me when I write? So much of my healing has taken place outside Jason's office, in the presence of God . . . even when I wasn't conscious of praying! I'm experiencing His counseling right *now*, in this journal entry as He responds to my prayer.

How far from God I've been all my life! But as my faith has grown, He has increased my faith even more through His response to me. It's what He promised: "Draw near to God and He will draw near to you" (Js. 4:8, NKJV). I had to have enough faith to believe He would answer me. I had to have ears to hear His answers. I had to be listening for Him.

I will still grieve losing the relationship with Jason. I've been dependent on him through so much pain that the thought of standing alone frightens my inner child. She still needs a physically present *person* to walk with her through the sorrow. *judy* is feeling an impending abandonment.

But an important part of what God is showing me here is that all human beings are always alone, when you come right down to it. God gives us mates and friends to fill up part of that aloneness, so we can share with someone. But eternity is between God and me.

My relationships are comforts God provides me. I need to cherish those relationships and care for them, but they exist *inside* my relationship with God, not separate from it. "for in Him we live and move and have our being" (Acts 17:28, NKJV).

God isn't asking me to quit therapy cold turkey. I have work to finish with Jason. But I won't be abandoned when the time comes to separate. I will still have Jesus, and that's a far more important relationship to hold on to. Thank you, Lord.

CHAPTER 12

Transference?
Not Me!! ————————————————●—

Marcel Proust wrote, "The real voyage of discovery consists not in seeking new landscapes, but in having new eyes."

The process of therapy had given me new eyes, and the landscape I saw unfolding within myself continued to disturb me with its dark complexity.

I examined in increasingly painful detail *judy's* understanding of what men expected of her. Her shame at this depth proved to be a generalized hopelessness that she could be valued for anything but sexuality.

Tuesday, May 1, 11:30 P.M.

Jason asked me again this afternoon if I had thought any more about a memory healing. But he didn't suggest a date to schedule it. Do I *need* another memory healing? I can't find much leftover shame about any of the flashbacks I've had. I don't feel any pressure to get it done, like I did the times before.

Later, when we were talking about the unhealthy "friendships" I've moved away from recently, Jason asked if any of them had been unhealthy friendships with men. "You mean the relationships I've *just* left behind?" I asked, puzzled.

"Whenever," he replied, shrugging his shoulders.

"Well," I began slowly, "I've had men friends. I guess I've been a caretaker with one or two, but not like the obsession with Tina's problem that brought me into counseling. They're like the other relationships that just don't seem to matter anymore. I'm more realistic about their unavailability to meet my needs, so I'm taking care of my needs without those relationships. I'm not chasing them anymore."

We went on to another topic of discussion, but I've come back to that fragment of conversation because I suddenly see that Jason was lighting another fuse. Here's the detonation. He asked if there had been any unhealthy relationships with men. He was offering me an opportunity to explore any relationships I regretted. He was asking me if I had ever committed adultery!

I understand where that question comes from. Victims of incest have had their boundaries damaged or demolished. Mine were pretty much destroyed. Add that to the fact that our relationships don't work because we don't know how to communicate our needs, and that our understanding of intimacy is confused. We're so angry inside, and so we're miserable.

There's an old country and western song that says, "Lonely women make good lovers." I guess we're pretty easy targets for men who are looking for sex without commitment. Even Christian women. We are prone to that kind of mistake because of our conditioning and our hunger for affirmation.

And Jason knows that my marriage has been struggling for years. Of course, I have denied that there was a problem, have pretended our relationship was perfect. (Who ever taught me to confront problems in a healthy way? I wonder now how we managed to stay married.)

Our relationship has degenerated into an angry, frustrated parent and a frightened, cringing child. He was always right and I was always wrong. Despite my husband's good qualities, I couldn't see him beyond *judy's* deep conviction that men are abusive and women are victims. Under my surface was rage.

But adultery? No, never *that*.

I have an uneasy feeling, though. Jason's question was another variation on the theme "Who were you in high school?" Both were gentle offers to explore the potential for sexual relationships other than marriage and incest. And both questions are based on the concept of transference.

Jason hasn't labeled any of my issues as transference. He doesn't use a lot of psychological jargon. But my psychology class last summer did address it briefly. Applying the label to the question of my adult sexual behavior is clarifying.

Transference is carrying forward the emotional responses to a person in a past experience (usually in childhood) and applying them unconsciously to a different person in a current situation that reminds us of the old event. Like the sudden panic attack that startled me recently when David neglected to shave before initiating sex. That fear wasn't about my husband! I instantly transferred my old response to my stepfather into the present relationship.

Transference has been speaking loud and clear in every personal interaction I've ever had, because of my old expectations of how I would be treated by men *and* women. *Don't expect to get your needs met! There is no justice, no recourse for unfair treatment. So look out for yourself. Defend yourself, because nobody else will. But put up a façade to make yourself look like the 'good' person they say you should be. Keep the secrets hidden, or people will know how bad you are.*

And especially, expect that you will be used, sexually and emotionally. The word no doesn't exist. Resistance is hopeless. With that transference of old emotional response in play, why would anyone be surprised that victims fall into repeated destructive sexual relationships?

But I didn't. Unless . . . unless I repressed something that happened with Ken, my first and only steady boyfriend before David. We dated for a full year, within the rigid structure my stepfather allowed. There was a whole lot of "making out," but that's where it ended. *Wasn't it?*

Maybe not. I remember at a drive-in movie once, he moved his hand up my thigh. Is that all? My memory ends there. But that piece of a memory is probably only a fragment of a complete picture that would show me in helpless compliance to whatever he chose to do.

Ken would have been surprised to discover I wasn't a virgin, contrary to my reputation. And he would have taken that as license to use my body. He would have interpreted my petrified silence to give consent. But he would have been wrong.

There is new grief at this unexpected loss. Even the public reputation I assumed was intact may have been an obvious lie to everyone else. Through transference, my family stole the last of my ragged shreds of dignity.

I am not ashamed. But I weep for the hopelessness of that fifteen-year-old girl. She never had the opportunity to hold her head up and know she was worthy of protection.

Wednesday, May 9, 2:00 A.M.

Yesterday Jason asked me, "How has your experience with men as a child affected your expectations of men in the present?"

I have to laugh and cry at the same time when I think that a couple of years ago I couldn't see any problem at all in the way I related to men. Denial kept the secret inside so I could survive it. But now I know what an enormous impact those old experiences had on my adult life.

We talked about another puzzle piece I've never examined—the influence of my natural father, Jack. Since the divorce when I was two, I've met him only twice.

He was passing through our hometown once and stopped to fill up at a gas station. Improbably, my mother happened to be driving by and recognized him. She pulled our car to a screeching halt and dragged his three children out to present us to him. She was shrill and accusatory, he was defensive. He'd had no intention to stop by and visit us.

Years later, when I was in high school, our family took one of our long driving trips through the state where Jack lives. Mom had stayed in touch with Jack's parents, so we stopped to visit them. By this time Carla and Gary had left home, so it was me alone of Jack's children to meet him for an ice cream soda. He rationalized that whole period of his life, saying he and Mom should never have gotten married. So I guess he was calling me a mistake.

judy, did you learn some lessons about men from Jack? Would you like to talk to him?

197

Yeah. Are you the one I was supposed to call "Daddy"? But you're the one who was never there. You showed me that daddies make babies with moms and then never notice that the babies even get born.

I learned you can't expect men to buy milk or shoes or houses for moms or for children. Moms have to do that by themselves because you can't find the daddy when kids are hungry.

All the daddy ever wanted anyway was to use some other woman's body to make himself feel good. When he does that, he gets to feel important. He gets to make the woman he has sex with feel bad and, at the same time, the mom and the children at home feel bad, too. So that makes him strong.

Men think they're great because their penises give them power over women. Making a baby means he controls the mom because she has to stay home with it to feed it and take care of it and then cook dinner and clean house. He can come home after being in bed with somebody else and put his feet up and yell at the mom for not being beautiful anymore and for being tired all the time and for being a witch and for never having enough money.

I hate you, Jack, for the crazy picture you gave me about men. You made a lot of big empty promises and then showed what a liar you were by leaving us. You never sent us any money. You never even picked up the phone.

You were the one who was missing when I cried and nobody held me. You were the one who should have known what my first words were and what my laugh sounded like when you carried me on your shoulders. You were the one who was missing when nobody taught me about the love between a husband and wife, or between a father and his child.

Because you were gone, there was no daddy ever to be proud of me when I went to the city spelling bee or to give me a special hug when I went on my first date. There was no daddy to give me away at my wedding or to be a grandfather to my children. You were never there for a birthday or a Christmas or any other day that was important to me. And it never occurred to you that you should be because you never gave me two minutes' worth of thought in all those years.

You showed me that daddies don't exist, and you showed me that I wasn't worth caring about. Lessons from you taught me to hate myself for not being good enough to be loved.

You left me behind without protection, to be raped all my life. And if you had been with us, you would have raped me, too. In spite of you, and the mess you left behind you, Jack, I have become who I am today. I am a woman that a real father would have been proud to have claimed as his daughter.

The healthier I become, the more loss it is to you for what you could have had in a relationship with me if you'd only cared. But you'll probably never understand that. I'm forgiving you, Jack, because I'm not willing to be chained to you anymore. You simply don't matter in my life. I leave you in God's hands.

Tuesday, May 15, 9:30 P.M.

I shared my processing about Jack in my session with Jason today. We talked about the contrast between what I experienced "daddies" to be, and what my daughters have experienced with David.

"Have you ever been jealous of your daughters, that they had a father?"

"Oh, no. I cherish the fact that they have had a father who's been there through all the years," I answered. How wonderful that there are *some* children who don't have to suffer through abandonment and rejection.

Saturday, May 19, 4:00 P.M.

As I jogged this morning, I mulled over the question of transference. Are there more ways my abuse has affected my expectations today? Yes. I've probably only scratched the surface.

Like my weight. Since I began running and addressed the eating disorder by giving up sugar, I've lost twenty-eight pounds. It helps that I'm running five miles pretty consistently now. I need to lose more, but I respect my body. I feel stronger, healthier.

Months ago Jason asked if my extra pounds were an effort to avoid being attractive, to avoid sexual attention. I denied it at the time. But now as I look at that issue in reverse, I discover that Jason was right. I've recognized that without the layer of protective fat, I find myself surprised that my husband can keep his hands off me. I've unconsciously anticipated increased sexual demands because I'm thinner.

So the opposite must be an unconscious expectation of decreased sexual demands when I'm heavier. My inner child was trying, in one more way, to say no when it wasn't permissible to say no. She thought maybe her body size could prevent the question from being asked. But even fat hasn't kept her safe.

I've seen for a long time that I've used food as a drug, to numb myself from uncomfortable feelings. Now whenever I see obese people on the street or in stores, I wonder what inner pain has driven them to wrap themselves in so much insulation.

I don't expect that my eating disorder will cease to be a struggle for me. But if *judy* can experience often enough that she can choose her own response to sexual situations, even with my husband, perhaps she'll be more comfortable with allowing the body size to be what it was intended to be. She has a right to say no, and I can back her up with boundaries instead of poundage.

Wednesday, May 23, 1:30 A.M.

Here's some writing I've tried to evade, but the topic is increasingly uncomfortable. I don't have any other means to get it out of my head than to write it down.

I canceled my therapy appointment yesterday. I had a cold, and all I wanted to do was sleep. But I've had colds before, and I kept my appointments anyway, because my commitment to therapy had a quality of desperation in it. I couldn't let go of my lifeline.

Was this cold truly a coincidence? I don't believe in coincidences anymore. There was a reason not to see Jason. I was avoiding him.

The previous week's session produced a question from Jason that shocked me by its directness. "Has the topic of sexual attraction ever come up between us?" My blood pressure went up, but wouldn't let myself feel it.

"No," I answered quickly and skirted the issue to address something more comfortable.

For a whole week I've pretended he didn't ask what he asked. So I'm still avoiding a painful issue I've never acknowledged, an issue that has existed for a long time. I'm still running away from confronting what's hard to acknowledge, like I've done all my life.

In a polite conversation with any other man I know, he would *not* ask me directly if I—a married woman!—were sexually attracted to him. But I don't have polite conversations with my counselor. Therapy goes beyond the polite to the honest. Honesty can be a very scary attribute to cultivate.

Why do I have to deal with this? If I had a woman counselor, I wouldn't have this assignment. I don't want to acknowledge what feels so shameful. *Should* it feel so shameful?

Is it bad to be attracted to a man who has been so attentive and concerned for my well-being? Is it a sin to be drawn to another human being who has supported me through the most intense grieving in my life? He knows all the ugly secrets I held inside for thirty years. And he accepts me, anyway. Is it shameful that I find something attractive in that?

Being with Jason is an experience of being "at home" for the first time in my life. I feel safe and protected. When I'm not with him, a part of me is so lonely for that feeling! There's an emptiness, a longing I can't quite define.

But he's married and has a family. And I'm married with a family. We're both moral, monogamous, Christian people with an entirely different purpose in mind. Neither of us is seeking a sexual relationship with the other. Why does it feel so *dangerous* all of a sudden? As if I were about to fall off a cliff!

Jason established very early in therapy that he recognized my vulnerability, and he promised not to be sexual with me. He said he wouldn't take advantage of my trust. Then where does this feeling come from, as if I expect that sexual demands will be made?

Wait. Where have I gotten all of my expectations about sexual behavior? From my past experience. Have I ever experienced a close relationship with a man that was *not* sexualized? No. *judy* can't quite believe a man could care about her and not ask her to be sexual. Besides that, why would *judy* believe any man's verbal promises that she is safe? Words are empty.

Will I ever reach the bottom of the pile of manifestations of the incest in my life? Will I grieve this confusion forever? Oh, no . . . there's more. I have to face the fact that it's more than just an expectation that Jason will ask for sex.

Now that I'm faced with the impending loss of the therapeutic relationship, *judy* is grasping at straws to hang on to a person she needs. She's afraid of abandonment, and by all her experience, sex is a way to hold on. Perhaps for her, being sexual wouldn't be too high a price to pay to keep Jason.

As much fear as that little girl had about sex, her need to be loved was vastly greater. Does this mean *judy* may have initiated some of the sexual behavior as a child? Probably. Poor child. She had real human needs to feel safe and valued. She needed touch and affection and nurturance and companionship. She needed to feel special to someone. She needed someone to acknowledge her existence. It isn't *bad* to want those things.

judy was conditioned to expect that none of those needs would be fulfilled anywhere outside the sexually abusive relationships. Experience taught her that her sexual behavior kept them coming back for more. She was able to create a sense of "belonging" that had never existed otherwise.

But the price tag was so high! For the hollow comfort of their attention, she sold her soul along with her body. And she's willing to make the same deal again to keep Jason, now that she's faced with losing him.

Oh, God! Of course I've been ashamed all my life! I'm ashamed now, that these feelings exist inside me!

I want to honor the nonsexual nature of the therapy relationship. I am committed to being faithful to my marriage vows. I respect Jason's integrity as a therapist and as a Christian and as a husband to his wife. But there is a force within me that has very different concerns. My boundaries are still so wobbly. Can I keep *judy* within the limits I set intellectually when she is so needy?

So this is where compulsions come from! This is the source of addictions, that irrational drive of a needy child to fill up the hole in her soul with whatever substance makes the pain go away! I've used food to numb that pain all my life. So many of us use alcohol and drugs. Sex is a powerful, addictive drug, too. I am resisting using any drug that isn't good for me.

But my inner child is throwing a tantrum on the floor. She wants what she wants because she wants it, and nobody better tell her any different! She's like a toddler who grasps a fascinating new toy—a shiny butcher knife. To be a loving parent to her, I must be willing to pry her clenched fingers from that blade. I have to be strong enough to listen to her screams and feel her kicking my shins, without giving in to what she thinks she wants.

Am I that strong? I honestly don't know. It would be so easy to relax and let her have her way. Then it would be up to Jason to say no. I hate to acknowledge this in myself, but I'm still not sure if I can be that firm with her.

So I'm praying for Jason's boundaries. *God, make him stronger than I am.*

Sunday, May 27, 11:00 P.M.

Maybe someday I'll get past the insomnia that has plagued me this year. I *am* getting more consistent sleep without waking than I used to. But since I can't get to sleep now, I'll record and clarify the insight I received while I was making dinner.

I was thinking about this new issue of attraction to Jason, which is another instance of transference. I suddenly saw that most of the shame is a direct result of the fact that the attraction seems to be sexual. At first glance that's a natural assumption. If an adult woman is attracted to an adult man, it must be a sexual attraction, right?

I'm very sure that sexual attraction *is* a big part of these "dangerous" feelings I'm struggling with. But maybe I assume too much to put all of those feelings into the same category as the results of sexual abuse.

After all, I do have other trauma from my childhood besides the incest—parental neglect being one. Before I began writing, I reread a few pages in Missildine's *Your Inner Child of the Past.* It confirmed my vague recollection of one of the effects of neglect.

Neglect creates, among other things, the effect of a sense of emptiness, an indefinable loss and longing, a *wanting* for something, we know not what. I think perhaps a large part of this desire *judy* has felt is in response to my neglect trauma.

From *Inner Child:* "The neglected 'inner child of the past' longs for the ultimate loving and complete acceptance which a mother gives her child." Missildine is talking about the most primal of losses—the loss of the bond between an infant and mother. Is some of the attraction to Jason aimed at the parent role a counselor fills?

Uh-oh. I wrote a couple of months ago that "what I want is a mother . . . someone who knows my story and accepts me for who I am, flaws and all." Then I said, "Wait. That's not a mother, that's a therapist. That's Jason."

Well, that's what Jason has been—someone who accepts me. But it *is* a description of a mother, or what a mother should be, anyway. So I've projected that onto Jason. I want him to be more than just my therapist. I've wanted Jason to be father/mother/higher power to me because each of those roles in my childhood was distant and abusive.

My inner child wants dependency because she was never allowed safe dependency when it was appropriate—in infancy and early childhood. *judy's* longing is a childlike wish to cling to a safe, nurturing parent.

Don't make me be grown-up! she pleads. *I've been grown-up all my life, and I don't want to anymore!*

But even with this recognition, the longing is still danger-ous . . . and sexual . . . because *judy* can't possibly have a clear understanding of the role of a healthy parent figure.

The meaning behind the word *father* is a confusing mixture of supporter, protector, user, betrayer, and sexual partner. What should be and what *is* are all mixed up in her mind.

How can she get that untangled? So the inner pressure to be sexual to hold onto the relationship is still in effect!

That leaves me where I was before. I'm at the mercy of Jason's boundaries (*judy* never knew a man who had boundaries). I'm afraid to trust him. I'm afraid to trust myself with him. That's why I canceled Tuesday's appointment, even though I wasn't conscious of it at the time.

Now that I've recognized it, I can't just ignore this. Jason raised the question of attraction between us because it was important to understand all of *judy's* expectations and needs. And I have learned that the more uncomfortable I am in addressing an issue, the more I *need* to address it. I will talk to Jason about my feelings about him. I won't run away from it.

Jason has been telling me for quite a while what a long distance I have come toward being healthy. I think I'm beginning to believe him. But won't it ever be easy?

Wednesday, May 30, 2:45 A.M.

Yesterday's session focused mostly on the transference between Jason and me. No matter that I was uncomfortable with the topic, Jason wasn't disturbed by it. He didn't assume I was out to rape him. It took a lot of the pressure off to have him confirm that these feelings are a natural consequence of the conditioning created by abuse, especially sexual abuse.

But one comment Jason made has brought some unsettling new thoughts. "I hope I haven't done anything to contribute to those 'dangerous' feelings you're experiencing. Therapists are human beings, too, and it's possible I may have made some mistakes in our work together that confused you. If so, I'm sorry."

In acknowledging his humanness, Jason gave me permission to confront him if his behavior had contributed to the problem. I can't see anything he's done that might have added to that burden, but how clear is my vision? My blind spot now is minuscule compared to the self-deception I used to live in. But I know there are still issues I can't identify.

One I *can* identify: *judy* isn't comfortable with the fact that Jason is a human being who makes mistakes. Underneath my intellectual awareness that no human being is perfect, is her terror of that reality. *Why can't he be perfect?*

My own perfectionism comes from my attempts to achieve some measure of control in the midst of the chaos of my family. I shame myself mercilessly for mistakes. Mistakes are a chink in the armor of perfection that *judy* sees as her only hope for survival. Her own mistakes seemed to make her vulnerable to more abuse.

Taking my therapist off the pedestal I constructed for him means he isn't perfect. So there's a fear that maybe he's just like all the other men *judy* knew as a child. Being emotionally vulnerable to an imperfect person means I'm at risk for abuse from the very man I need so desperately to trust.

Of *course* I need to recognize that therapists aren't perfect. But the illusion that he *is* perfect exists because I needed to trust *someone*. I could never believe in the balance of a person who can be both flawed *and* trustworthy. Nobody in my childhood was trustworthy. Even David, for all his good qualities, has wounded me over the years. *judy* hopelessly added his name to the list of abusers—he was sexual with me. So she removed her trust.

I had to believe in Jason's perfection, or I would have been too afraid to trust him. I needed the illusion first, even though it set me up to suffer a loss when I could finally come to grips with the reality that Jason, like everyone else, has feet of clay.

This is the same grief that children should experience very young. In functional families, a child comes to terms with the parent as loving and accepting, yet sometimes unfair and uncomprehending of the child's pain. Through all that, the child of a healthy family learns to retain her belief in the parent's basic trustworthiness.

I still believe intellectually in Jason's trustworthiness. But *judy* is afraid. She thought she was bonding with someone she had proved infallible through a series of little "tests" during the process of therapy.

He passed the tests. Within the role of counselor, Jason has responded to me in consistently supportive ways, even while he has challenged me to face painful facets of my life. He knew I was strong enough to confront my old shame.

But as well as Jason knows me, I know so little about him personally! If I'm going to let him be a human being, step down off the pedestal, *judy* needs to know he's a safe human being.

Human beings make mistakes that are related to the unresolved wounds they carry. I know that from my own life. I need to find a way to accept him as he is, knowing he has his own set of wounds, in order to trust Jason enough to depend on his boundaries and finish therapy with him. But Jason is a *man!*

Women therapists, too, are human beings, and sometimes abuse clients. But for a victim of incest with a history of abuse by male parent-figures, her vulnerability with a male parent-figure therapist is exponentially higher than with a woman. A victim's ability to say no is guaranteed to be more greatly damaged in an intimate situation with a man.

And the unconscious vibes her inner child sends out to a male parent-figure could be interpreted by a wounded, needy male therapist as a sexual invitation. There is already the natural dynamic of sexual attraction when working on intimate issues with a member of the opposite sex.

Deep therapy work requires us to lay down our old boundaries that surround "speaking the secret." We are at our most defenseless in a powerfully bonded relationship with a counselor. Some therapists have weak boundaries and gratify their own needs with clients. It's an all too common story of revictimization, a new incidence of incest with a parent-figure.

No one ever taught us to make objective judgments about a therapist's trustworthiness. We can't see their motives until it's too late. Some of them *are* safe. Jason must be, or he would have taken advantage of me already. But every one of them is human, and we—victims of abuse—often can't tell them apart.

Paradoxically, I believe I was led to Jason. I can't explain it, but I can't ignore the fact that God has done an amazing healing in my life, using Jason as His hands to minister to me. God didn't wait until Jason was perfect before He blessed others through him. God won't wait until I'm perfect, either, before He works through my life to touch others.

Could it be that God has shown me this question of Jason's imperfection because He's teaching me to accept and trust *myself*, even though I'm an imperfect person? Doesn't God accept me and Jason, too, with all our flaws?

Nobody's perfect. Do you hear that, *judy*? We are never going to be perfect in this life. Maybe if you can accept and trust Jason as imperfect, you can accept yourself. You can forgive yourself for mistakes you will continue to make as long as you are a human being.

So how is that trust for Jason going to be restored? It will have to be on faith. God has shown me the purpose of the exploration, and He'll give me the grace to trust Jason. I've learned that when He shows me His will, He always backs me up with the means to follow through in the action He asks of me. Trust. And finish the healing.

Oh . . . is this diminished trust the reason behind the fact that I haven't felt any pressure to do a final memory healing? Maybe, instead, *judy* has been resisting going back there because it requires so much trust in the man who's going to lead me. But Jason has already proven himself trustworthy, hasn't he? Yes.

Thank you for the lesson, Lord. I leave it to you to restore my confidence. You're in charge of my human counselor, too. Strengthen his boundaries and mine, and keep us both safe.

CHAPTER 13

Healing the Shame ———————◆●

I couldn't be sure that what I thought was the deepest of wounds was, in fact, the final need for healing. I couldn't guarantee that my most painful work was finished. But the time seemed suddenly to be right; I was ready to take it before God. Perhaps there would be more to do later.

Thursday, June 7, 8:00 A.M.

I awoke from a grisly dream this morning, hyperventilating and repelled by the graphic image I experienced.

I dreamed I was in the rest room at church, talking to my friend Kate. She was invisible behind the partition, in the stall next to mine. We were both menstruating, and she joked about how big an imposition periods are for her. I agreed emphatically.

Our conversation began as easy sardonic banter. But it soon developed into a heated outcry of our mutual frustrations about our powerlessness over ovaries and uteruses. Our reproductive systems, with the messy functions they perform of their own apparent volition, are burdens we would both gladly relinquish.

Then I was alone. Kate was gone and the rest room was empty, hushed and cold. Washing my hands, I was taken by surprise in a sudden wave of weakness. My knees buckled and I sank, frightened and dizzy, to the sterile whiteness of the tile floor.

A silent trickle of blood appeared from between my legs. I stared stupidly as it began to pool beneath me, warming the chill ceramic surface. I wanted to cry out, to stop the flow that soaked my skirt and caked around my calves and heels. But I was mute, helplessly observing in horror as the red stream increased in volume.

Despite my desperation to stanch the flow, an impulse to push, like that final stage of childbirth, irresistibly urged me to bear down. I delivered only clots of blood, pushing, pushing out larger and larger clumps until they emerged, looking like enormous chunks of raw liver. Pieces of myself. But still the flow increased. I was hemorrhaging, prostrate in a lake of blood.

The room began to tilt and swirl around me, and the last of my energy ebbed away. *"How can I lose so much blood and still live?"* I thought in panic and jerked awake with a start.

And now I consciously ask: How could I reject so integral a part of myself and still live? *judy* has given me a clear vision of her wish to rid herself of her hated femaleness! It was an ironic choice to cast my friend Kate in the supporting role in my dream. She had a complete hysterectomy years ago, when she was in her early twenties. She has in reality succeeded in ridding herself of several representative parts of her femaleness. Hysterectomies are common to victims. What dysfunction lies behind Kate's self-destructing uterus?

I haven't lived out that self-destructive impulse in "female problems." Instead, that core of shame festered deep inside while I whitewashed the blackness of my real opinion of myself. Oh, I was a great actress! I always wore a perfectly detailed mask with a wide smile. I was an exemplary friend, supporter, leader, teacher, helper. I focused on anyone but myself. I couldn't maintain the *act* if the camera focused on me.

judy couldn't tolerate the fearful possibility that others might recognize her for what she truly believed herself to be. If she lost control of the situation and her mask was ripped away, she'd be publicly exposed as a hideous, misshapen monstrosity—a female!

Inhabiting a female body defined me as responsible for the sex I couldn't prevent, didn't it? "Double bind" is a phrase Jason has used before to label an untenable role I was required to fill. It seems far too weak an expression for the craziness of this disgust for my own flesh. There were a hundred different locks on *this* bind I was in.

I always disdained Sigmund Freud's notion of female "penis envy." Why would I ever have wanted one of *those*? No, even in my most painful honesty, I can't believe I ever harbored a wish to possess that dreaded appendage. But perhaps Freud misidentified a very real longing not to be female. Perhaps being a violent male oppressor would be the lesser evil over the inescapable despair of female existence as I saw it. I was both helpless, hopeless victim, and evil seductress.

This, then, must be the bottom of the well. This pain is far more profound than the shame for any specific event in my past. Can there be any deeper injury than the ultimate humiliation of despising my own existence within the female gender?

What cruelty lay behind God's decision to make me this way? Does all of heaven laugh at the burlesque of a female attempting to survive this male-oriented world in a body booby-trapped with all the wrong parts? Females are nothing more than a central *hole*—I shudder at that word! We have a void of soft mucous membrane where hard muscle and bone should be!

We are only receptacles, empty waste containers to be filled with the slime men rid themselves of. My inner child long ago internalized the summation of the female sex in an exchange I overheard between two teenage boys one summer: "Just look at all the *gash* on this beach!" Her reality was exactly that—an identity as *gash*, and nothing else.

It should surprise no one that militant feminists are so angry at the male-female inequities of the social system. They're dug in for battle, flashing their claws and baring sharpened fangs. Perhaps their defensive rage at being so victimized harkens back to a common core of revulsion for femaleness itself. None of us were ever offered the opportunity to sign up for the male gender. We never had options.

214

I see at last the true reason why Bear, representative of my inner child, has always been a he. Maleness, while hated and feared, was still unquestionably preferable to the abomination of femaleness with all its pitiable connotations. If *judy* had no hope of being any less a victim, then grant at least this one wish—let Bear, at least, be not-female.

God help me.

Friday, June 15, 11:30 P.M.

In my session yesterday, I confessed my long-suppressed body and gender shame. Jason displayed his usual acceptance and empathy. I felt reasonably comfortable in trusting him, even with such a sensitive self-disclosure. But I can't help thinking that Jason, for all his skill and gift as a counselor, cannot fully comprehend the depth of this shame. Jason can't heal it. But I'm praying that God will.

In keeping with that prayer, rather than assuming that Jason will tell me when the final memory healing will be, I requested that we schedule it for next week. We planned two consecutive hours next Friday. It's time, finally.

The right timing required that I bring to the surface the concerns that needed healing. Body shame wasn't apparent to me until I finally saw inside that last wall of self-deception. Without honestly identifying the injury, it can't be healed.

The other item on the list for healing is something I've recognized as a recurrent theme as I have reread my journal. I need to be healed of the wound from Mother's emotional abandonment. It still holds a surprising amount of pain.

And in order to face the pain with Jason beside me, I had to be sure of my trust for Jason. That trust seems to be restored. I can't see any leftover qualms there. So I'm ready to move on.

Tuesday, June 19, 2:00 A.M.

Unexpectedly, I had another new issue show up. At the mall yesterday, I browsed through the recovery section in a bookstore. A bookstore is one of my favorite places. Books have always been a comfort to me. How strange that such a strong extrovert as myself has spent so much of her life alone, curled into a corner with a book. I sought safety in solitude and answers in the printed word.

That sense of safety evaporated yesterday. I turned from the self-help shelves and was confronted, on the facing wall, with an array of volumes about sexuality. I had a sudden impulse to buy a sex therapy book, one that might help me to deal with some of the difficulties in my sexual relationship with my husband.

But holding those books in my hands and skimming them in order to choose one, I became conscious of looking over my shoulder to see who might be witnessing the heinous crime I was committing. I felt my anxiety level rise dramatically.

Anxiety? The recognition came as a surprise. Of the 150 or so recovery and spirituality books I've read in the past year and a half, several dozen have related to sexual abuse and sexual healing. Has this anxiety been present through all that reading without my awareness of it? Have I been as numb as that?

I suppose my generalized anxiety through this whole gut-wrenching process of therapy has been so high that I might not have consciously acknowledged the source of the additional discomfort. True to my standard form, I bulled my way through some very heavy reading, books I chose in spite of Jason's cautions not to overload myself. Is it possible *judy* needed me to draw a boundary to exclude some of that threatening material I kept on inhaling like cocaine? I can finally hear her uneasiness.

What if somebody sees me holding this book, or buying it? They'll know I want sex! They'll know I like it! They'll know I do those nasty things!"

Wait a minute. Is there something known as objective reality on this topic? I think I can recognize that *judy's* viewpoint on sex is confused, in natural response to the abuse. But what is "normal"? I still don't know.

Intellectually, I believe what I have read and what Jason has emphasized—sexual union between a husband and wife is ordained by God. Pleasure is an intended part of the design.

But the voice in my head disagrees. She sees buying a book dealing with maximizing sexual satisfaction as *asking* for sexual pleasure. She's right. And the idea is horrifyingly shameful!

But, *judy*, it's okay to ask for pleasure. It's okay to communicate sexual needs. Sexual pleasure bonds a husband and wife together as one. God didn't intend sex just to make babies, but for our enjoyment. It's a gift He gave you.

But I never asked for it! I never wanted it! God gave me something He must have meant for somebody else. It doesn't fit, I don't want it, I don't like having those bad feelings! If God wanted to give me a present, couldn't He have given me something else— warm socks, or . . . a book? Anything . . . anything but that!

Oh, child, how they hurt you! I can't argue away this stubborn conviction. God will have to heal this shame. Perhaps we'll have time to include it in the memory healing session on Friday. There must be a reason He's shown it to me now.

Friday, June 22, 9:00 P.M.

In spite of my emotional exhaustion, I need to record today's healing session. I can't sleep until I write how God was with us in the counseling office.

As I entered, Jason saw my fear beneath the mask of determined calm. To put me at ease, he began the session by reading from *The Living Bible*—a psalm of David, about confession. I looked it up just now, to record the words that prepared me for the experience. "What happiness for those whose guilt has been forgiven! What joys when sins are covered over! What relief for those who have confessed their sins and God has cleared their record.

"There was a time when I wouldn't admit what a sinner I was. But my dishonesty made me miserable and filled my days with frustration. All day and night your hand was heavy on me. My strength evaporated like water on a sunny day until I finally admitted all my sins to you and stopped trying to hide them. I said to myself, 'I will confess them to the Lord.' And you forgave me! All my guilt is gone.

"Now I say that each believer should confess his sins to God when he is aware of them, while there is time to be forgiven. Judgment will not touch him if he does.

"You are my hiding place from every storm of life; you even keep me from getting into trouble! You surround me with songs of victory. I will instruct you (says the Lord) and guide you along the best pathway for your life; I will advise you and watch your progress. . . .

"Many sorrows come to the wicked, but abiding love surrounds those who trust in the Lord. So rejoice in him, all those who are his, and shout for joy, all those who try to obey him" (Ps. 32:1–8, 10–11, TLB).

I relaxed a little in that clear promise of God's faithfulness to cleanse us if we will only open our hearts to Him. Memory healing is exactly that—allowing ourselves to be honest and open before God. I've come such a long way to trust God with honesty about my innermost shame.

Then Jason read James 5:13–16, from the *Modern Language Bible*: "Is any of you suffering trouble? Let him pray. Is anyone feeling cheerful? Let him sing psalms. Is anyone of you ill? Let him call the elders of the church, and let them pray for him and in the name of the Lord anoint him with olive oil. The prayer of faith will restore the sick one, and the Lord will raise him up. And if he has committed sin, it will be forgiven him. Therefore confess your sins to each other and pray for one another, that you may be cured. The earnest prayer of a righteous person has great effect."

I have been ill. I've been sick at heart all these years, tortured by a thorn in the flesh I could never overcome on my own. Yet I was afraid to expose that thorn by asking for help. Those verses calmed my fears and reaffirmed my own belief in prayer. God is in the business of healing. And so we began—in prayer.

Jason asked God to hear everything we said today as He had heard all the sessions that had gone before, as a prayer of confession of my deep pain from old wounds. As he prayed, he claimed on my behalf God's promise of healing for those who trust in Him. Then he asked the Lord, whose presence is not limited by time or space, to go with us to a time before my conscious memory.

As Jason began to speak, he seemed to be addressing me, yet I knew that he was acutely conscious of God's closeness, just as I was. The Lord was listening to the words with a concentration greater than my own. Perhaps He even provided the words I needed to hear.

"*judy*, there was a time, before you were born, when your parents had no knowledge of what you would be like. At the instant that an egg and a sperm joined together to begin a developing new life, your mother and father had no awareness of the miracle uniting cells from their two bodies.

"But God was present and aware of the meaning in that event. You came into being by God's own purpose, through the action of Jesus. The Living Bible's paraphrase of John 1:3

is speaking of Jesus when it tells us: 'He created everything there is—nothing exists that He didn't make.' As He made you, *judy*.

"Even then, Jesus had already known you, before He laid the foundations of the earth and created the stars in the heavens. From the beginning there had been a plan for the texture of your hair, the color of your eyes, the tone of your voice, and a million other details that defined your individuality. He could see, even then, the person He longed for you to become, the person you are becoming even now. He made you for the pleasure of knowing you. He created you especially to be adopted as His own dearly loved child.

"You developed from a fertilized egg into an embryo and then a fetus, with distinct body parts promising the form of your eventual completion. He oversaw the growth of fingers and toes and inner organs, specialized to accomplish their own necessary functions in sustaining your life. As you grew within your mother's body, the Lord was pleased that your time had begun.

"According to His intention for you from the very first, God directed the formation of ovaries to determine that you would be female. He bathed you in a perfect hormonal balance of a fluid designed to nourish your growth as a girl-child, because that's what He wanted you to be.

"Within your mother's womb, He formed your body to include a uterus and a vagina. Even while you were yet so tiny, He instilled messages within your brain to be transmitted years later. At the perfect time of your life, those messages would direct the glands in your body to release hormones that would change you from a girl-child into a physically mature woman. His blueprint for your sexuality was complete, even in the womb.

"As the time for your birth grew near, the Lord surveyed what He had made, and He saw that it was very good. God's

220

design for you and His intentions for you were perfect. But those months of growth inside your mother's body weren't free from the impact of the world outside, were they, *judy*?"

I was so transfixed, in awe of the scene Jason had painted for me, that I had to rouse myself to answer at last, "*No*." *judy* resisted letting go of the beautiful image of God's creative energy in her life to look instead at the pain of family influence.

But Jason continued, drawing me firmly to more unpleasant images I needed to see. "We know that every growing fetus receives physical and emotional messages from the mother's own life and environment. Were the circumstances of your mother's life during that time happy, *judy*?"

I shook my head. Jason already knew the answer to that question.

"No. It wasn't a time of tranquility for her. And your mother's stress was transmitted to the child inside her. In the warm darkness that surrounded you, your consciousness must have begun with the rhythm of your mother's heartbeat and the movement of her body.

"Every sound that your ears received was filtered through the steady rushing of blood pulsing through her uterine walls and the predictable inhale-exhale of the air in her lungs. But in the midst of those sounds that signified life itself, there were, without warning, startling invasions of the essential calm of your environment.

"From your earliest awareness, muffled shouts and cries sporadically disturbed your sleep. However much your infant mind craved peace and security in which to develop as God intended, you were powerless to stop the frightening clamor that repeatedly assaulted your ears. You felt your mother's panic, and your own.

"The motion of your mother's activities could lull you into a comfortable twilight, but sometimes, when the terrible noise began again, there were sudden, jarring movements, blows that threatened to crush you. The physical violence erupting on the outside of your world pitched the audible discord into a level that filled you with terror. You were screaming. From before your birth."

How could Jason know all this? judy thought. *It was never safe, even before I was born!* By this time, tears were running down my face, in confirmation of everything Jason had said.

"Do you have any words, *judy*, for the feelings you must have experienced in the midst of that chaos?" Jason asked me gently.

"It was . . . all mixed up! I was . . . afraid. And there was . . . rage! But I couldn't . . ." I choked to a halt, inarticulate.

"You were powerless?" Jason offered.

I nodded miserably.

"Were you hopeless, even then?"

"Yes," I whispered, blowing my nose.

"Yes. And then, again without warning, there was a new kind of pain. You were being squeezed from every side, without letup. Over and over again, your whole body was strangled in the grip of muscles tightening, pushing you into an unfamiliar passage. For hours, you were battered, constricted and paralyzed, enraged and afraid.

"Then suddenly, horrifyingly, you were thrust out of the close dark warmth that was all you had known since the beginning. Now there was only an open place of dazzling, glaring light, piercing noise, and cold air. For the first time, you voiced your pain with a loud cry of your own.

"But there was no comfort. You had foreign objects thrust into your mouth and nose, and a sharp prick in your foot brought blood and more pain. Even your mother's heartbeat was gone. It was the time of your birth, *judy*. Was this new place any safer than where you had been?"

"No," I whispered. *"I was never safe."*

"Did you know, *judy*, that there was someone present at your birth who wanted to make you safe then?"

"*Was ... Jesus there?*" I asked wistfully.

"He was there all along. I think if you look at that scene again, you'll find Him peering over the doctor's shoulder. Can you see Him, *judy*?"

"*Yes.*"

"Can you see the nurse wrap you in a blanket as she takes you from the doctor's arms?"

I nodded.

"She's laying you in a warming bassinet, and the doctor is turning his attention back to your mother. But Jesus has moved to stand next to your bassinet, and He's looking down at you. Is there something you'd like Jesus to do, *judy*?"

I didn't wait for Jason's prompting this time. "*Will you hold me, Jesus?*"

My heart was so full of longing and hope as I watched Jesus reach into the little bed and scoop my newborn baby self into His arms. "*But does He really want me?*" I said through my tears.

"Why don't you ask Him?"

I looked into His face and said, "*Do you want me, Jesus?*"

Jesus smiled, crinkling the corners of His eyes. Then, cupping my head in the palm of His hand, He laid me against His chest, enclosing me completely in His arms. I heard His voice, whispered into my ear, rumbling through His chest. "Yes! It's you I want. I made you with this in mind. I chose you to be my own child." He rocked me slowly back and forth.

I was safe. I was wanted. I was loved. Just for who I am.

Jason interrupted the moment by asking quietly, "Jesus does want you, *judy*. Is He holding you now?"

I nodded, amused at the surprising confirmation that Jason doesn't have any magic. He couldn't see the scene I was experiencing.

"Can you hear Jesus' heartbeat?"

"*Yes.*" Cradled against His chest, I listened to the sound reverberating in my ear.

"Jesus can be the parent you never had as a child, *judy*. You are in His care, now and for always. He's promised you that. Now that you're safe with Him, let Jesus carry you out of the delivery room. He's still holding you close, wrapped warm in a blanket against Him. He's walking down the hallway, through the glass doors, and outside into the night. Jesus wants you to know how much He loves you."

Jason began to sing softly to me, "Jesus loves me, this I know, for the Bible tells me so." Then he said, "Do you know the words, *judy*?"

I struggled to get out any sound at all, barely able to whisper along with him through my tears as he sang, "Little ones to him belong, they are weak, but He is strong. Yes, Jesus loves me . . ."

After that, Jason invited me to come back gradually into the office again. I returned as the adult me, with a sense of relief and the emotional depletion that comes of intense effort expended. Jason encouraged me to relax for a few minutes. There was more work ahead.

We exchanged awed comments about the experience. I drank some water and resettled myself in my chair for another trip back through the years.

"Is your inner child ready to look at another memory?" Jason asked.

I took a breath. "Okay."

"We've both agreed that the wound from your mother's emotional abandonment is one that we need to address," Jason began. "Is there a particular incident that comes to mind as being representative of that pattern that existed between you for years?"

"My eighth birthday," I said without hesitation. It was more than a year ago that I had first told Jason about that memory.

Jason nodded. "The birthday cake. If you close your eyes, *judy*, can you see the kitchen?"

"*Yes.*"

"Tell me what you see and what happened there."

I took a deep breath and described for him in detail the room and the family gathered around the table. Sarcastic verbal jibes from Gary, as he wolfed down his food. Mother's face, as always, worn and tired, impatient with the ever-present strife among us. Carla and my little brother, Will, eating quietly, resolutely.

But all during the meal, the cake—that perfect confection whose existence was an affirmation of my value—called to me from the counter across the room. It positively sang: "You are worth angel food cake soaked with the juice of the sweetened strawberries, slathered with the lightest whipped cream!"

I finished my supper. Meat loaf. Green beans. Mashed potatoes with butter. I ran my finger around the plate methodically, licking away the last of the crumbs I scooped up. Only when the plate sparkled was it finally prepared for what was to come: my birthday cake.

But that didn't happen.

"When your mother served the cake, who got the first piece?" Jason asked when I paused at the climax of the story.

"*Gary did.*" Gary, who took my mother's attention and Carla's allegiance—Gary, who hurt me all my life! Mom gave *him* the first piece of my cake. And I got nothing.

"What do you want to say to your mother?" asked Jason.

"But Mother, I didn't get a piece of my birthday cake!" Struggling to hold back my tears, it came out as a little-girl whine.

"What else didn't you get from your mother?"

"Attention. Love . . . she never loved me."

"No. She didn't love you. She didn't listen to you. And she didn't believe you about the cake."

"No. She said, 'Don't lie to me to get another piece of cake! I gave you the first piece and you ate it already!'" Tears dripped off my chin. I blew my nose.

"And no one defended you?"

I shook my head. *"There was never anyone to defend me. Nobody cared."*

"I believe we can change that image, *judy*," Jason said quietly. "Why don't we back up, to the moment just before your mother served the cake. As she stands to get the cake from the countertop, you can see yourself push back your chair, stand up, and walk to the front door. Open the door. Is someone waiting there?"

I smiled. *"It's Jesus."*

"Do you think He'd like to come in?"

I nodded.

"Invite Him inside."

"Come in, Jesus," I whispered.

"Let Him take your hand and walk with you into the kitchen. As both of you stop beside the table, Mom is turning around with the cake plate in her hands. Can you see her surprise as she notices who's with you?"

"She almost dropped the plate!"

"Let's let Jesus take the cake plate out of her hands. He can set it down on the table in front of you. Now, as Jesus is making eye contact with Mom, can you describe the look on His face?"

"He's disappointed. He's . . . stern."

"He's disappointed in the way she has treated you. Is He angry that she let you be hurt?"

I nodded.

"How does He feel about you, *judy*?"

"*He loves me. He wants to protect me.*"

"That's why He's with you now. He won't let her hurt you anymore. But now that He's protecting you, can you tell me what your mother is feeling?"

I looked at her face and saw all her hopelessness. "*She's afraid. Ashamed. She's ashamed like me.*"

"Does your mother need forgiveness, *judy*?"

I nodded. I was ready for this step.

"Can you let Jesus forgive your mother?"

"*Yes.*"

"What would Jesus want you to say to your mother?"

I took a deep breath. "*I forgive you, Mama.*"

"That *is* what Jesus would want. He's seen your resentment hold you in bondage to the memory of your birthday for too many years. Forgiving your mother is one step you've needed to take to release you from that. Does anyone else need forgiveness for what's happened here?"

"*Me,*" I whispered.

"You've hurt Jesus by keeping yourself bound by your bitterness to that old wound. God has been grieved that you have held yourself back from becoming the whole, healthy person He created you to be, for letting your hatred fill you up, keeping His love out. Will you ask Him for His forgiveness for that?"

I nodded and focused on Jesus' face. His expression was one of such anguish, mixed with love. I could see how much I had hurt Him. "*Forgive me, Lord,*" I said. "*I didn't mean to hurt you.*" He put His arms around me and drew me close to Him.

"Has He forgiven you, *judy*?" Jason asked softly.

It took me a few minutes to compose myself enough to answer. I blew my nose. "*Yes. He forgives me.*"

"Have you forgiven yourself, Judy?"

The adult me was responsible for this one. "I haven't before. But I forgive myself now."

"Good. Jesus has been waiting for this day for too long. It's time you found peace.

"Do you think if you ate some birthday cake with Jesus that it would set you back in your sugar addiction? I know you're abstinent now."

I smiled. "I guess Jesus can do anything. He can make it sugar-free!"

"Good. Because now I think He wants you to have your birthday cake. As He begins to cut the cake, *judy*, why don't you get two clean dessert plates from the cabinet?"

Grinning in spite of myself, I watched myself climb onto a chair to fetch two plates from the good dishes on the top shelf. And two clean forks.

"Jesus has cut two very big pieces of cake, with extra strawberries and whipped cream. He's putting the cake onto the plates you've brought. He's handing you one plate, and He picks up the other plate in his right hand. Let Him take your right hand with His left, and together you can walk to the front door and go outdoors, carrying your cake. Would you like to climb your tree with Jesus?"

I nodded.

"Who's going first?"

"*Jesus. He's taking off His sandals, and I'm holding His cake while He climbs up.*"

"Who told Him to take off His sandals?"

"*Nobody. He knows you have to be barefoot to climb a mulberry tree!*"

"I guess He's climbed trees before. When He's settled on the branch, He can take the cake and let you climb up to join Him. Let me know when you're comfortable."

I watched myself balance on the branch and lean back against the trunk. Then I nodded to Jason. Jesus handed me my cake with a smile.

"Before you eat it," Jason broke in, "there's a surprise for you up on that fluffy cloud that just passed in front of the moon."

I looked up through the leaves of my tree and saw the cloud, luminous with the moonlight that shone through it. And as Jason described the scene, a choir of angels, all in white, appeared. When they were assembled, Amy Grant led them in a chorus of "Happy Birthday to You." Jesus held my hand.

And I let myself cry.

CHAPTER 14

Aftershocks

How amazing to see that the same person (me!) who struggled, just a few months before, to believe in a God who would answer prayer was waiting for Him to show up with a miracle. My faith was a gift, from God's gentle leading into gradually deeper and deeper waters of belief. I had experienced His involvement in my life. I knew He would finish the work.

Saturday, June 23, 11:30 A.M.

I find myself waiting for the other shoe to drop. The healing session yesterday was wonderful, but...incomplete. We didn't have time—or insight enough—to heal everything. I'm waiting for God to do something more. I'm listening in anticipation of a voice I don't hear yet.

In *Healing of Memories*, David Seamands cites numerous cases when God provided even more dramatic healings after "official" memory healing sessions. Like "aftershocks."

Will that happen for me? I asked Jason about that possibility at the end of that amazing session yesterday.

He shrugged and said, "Not everyone experiences it in the same way. But I don't want to limit God to what I'm able to accomplish."

So the answer is maybe. In the meantime, to deal with this impatience I'm feeling while I wait for what might not happen anyway, I gave myself an assignment. Looking for a standard to help me define the word *normal*, I've been through all the Bible references in my concordance that refer to the word *pleasure*.

It occurred to me this morning that the meaning of *pleasure* was confused because of my history. *judy* seems to have taken sexual pleasure out of the context of any other kind of pleasure that humans experience. But now I'm thinking that all variations of pleasure exist on a continuum of sorts.

God has pleasure. It's one of the ways humans are made in His image. Among other things, He has pleasure in our uprightness (1 Chr. 29:17), in the prosperity of His servants (Ps. 35:27), and in those who hope in His mercy (Ps. 147:11).

It is His "good pleasure" to give us the kingdom (Luke 12:32). We were created (along with everything else) for God's pleasure (Rev. 4:11).

Taking it one step further, it was interesting that a number of references used the words "God's pleasure" to mean "God's will"! The *King James Version* of Ezra 10:11, for example, says, "make confession . . . and do His pleasure." The same verse in the *Modern Language Version* says, "and do His will." Psalm 103:21 in the *King James* says "Bless ye the Lord . . . ye ministers of His . . . that do His pleasure." In the *New International Version*, the meaning is translated: "who do His will."

I'm still very confused here. Okay, it's easy to say that God is pleased if we do His will. I guess if the same original Hebrew word can be translated variously as God's pleasure and as God's will (intention, perfect design, purpose), I am forced to acknowledge that pleasure is good. At least God's pleasure is good. (*judy's* still fighting me here.)

But what about human pleasure? Pleasure is not only defined as arousal due to sexual stimulation." Don't we experience pleasure at the sight of a radiant sunset, at the gurgle of a baby's laughter, or in the comfort of a trusted friend's embrace?

As a parent, I take pleasure in my children. I have a psychological-emotional-physiological experience of goodness (pleasure) in response to my daughters' expressions of love for me. God designed us to be, like Him, beings who feel pleasure at a positive event or circumstance.

The God who designed the flashing iridescence of a tiny hummingbird's wings or the impossibly sweet scent of orange blossoms or the peaceful sigh of a breeze whispering through pine trees, had to mean it all for our enjoyment: pleasure. How have we become so numb to the goodness of God?

The same God who made the stars in the heavens, the Grand Canyon, and the Pacific Ocean, not to mention furry kittens and the taste of fresh pineapple, birdsong, butterflies, honeybees, and a billion other beautiful things that give me pleasure, also made me. He created my body, my *whole* body. I think my inner child believed He must have left blank spots that Satan filled in with evil genitalia. But God is responsible for all the goodness of human sexuality, too. (Yes, *judy*, *goodness*!)

He might have chosen to implant the drive to propagate our species as a horrible compulsion, to provide a brief respite from inner pain. Instead, He gave us a gentle sensation of tenderness that blossoms into delicious arousal, culminating in a joyous release of exquisite tension. He made it feel so good because He meant it to be good. He meant that goodness to draw us into oneness with our life partners.

(Surprise! Even in the semantics that flow from the tip of my pen here, there seems to be an intertwined relationship between various forms of the word *goodness*, and that which is pleasing, pleasant and pleasurable! The dictionary and thesaurus confirm it.)

God is glorified by my experience of pleasure as a recognition that something He created is good. Most of the time we fail to give God credit, but each sensation of pleasure is intended as a cue to praise Him as the source of the good gift that produces that enjoyment.

Yet how many people are comfortable enough with sexuality to invite God's presence into their bedrooms? This is opposite to *judy's* lifelong belief, but I recognize intellectually that God would surely be pleased if we could trust Him enough to ask His blessing on our times of lovemaking. If I tell *judy* that it's okay to ask for pleasure, can't I tell her that it's *good* to ask God to teach the trust that would enhance sexual pleasure? And that it's *good* to praise Him for orgasms? She's still aghast at the idea.

God is there, watching, anyway. He's known all along what goes on under the sheets. But our sinful society has so warped our understanding of sexuality that, in our shame, we unconsciously deny His awareness of it.

Like children sneaking cookies from the cookie jar, enjoying just as much of this bad, guilty excitement as we can clutch in our grubby little hands, we keep watch over our shoulders to make sure we aren't being observed in our sin. We children never knew that those cookies were baked just for us. God wants us to savor them.

A healthy lifetime monogamous sexual relationship is protective of our emotional vulnerability. At the same time, it encourages the trust that frees us for ecstatic sexual abandonment. But most of us treat the marriage bed, ordained by God and "undefiled" (Heb. 13:4 NKJV), as a family secret. What we call privacy is more often an inability to be frankly verbal about sexual needs, even with our mates. We can't say the words! Unconsciously, we've bought the line about the "badness" of sex. But He meant it for good.

The Lord doesn't want me to waste the goodness of the sexual feelings He created in me. My stubborn resistance to a grateful acceptance of the gift of sexuality is victory for my abusers, not the determined insistence of purity *judy* meant it to be. She always misunderstood. She was confused.

William Cowper might have been referring to a sexual abuser when he said he "stamps God's own name upon a lie just made." It was sin, not God, that imposed the shame around sexual feelings.

I can still feel her resistance, but I will not let *judy* live out her days in submission to that lie. The truth will set her free.

Saturday, June 23, 10:00 P.M.

This afternoon I recognized another piece of insight to heal *judy's* sexual shame. Sexual perversion inflicts what we might arguably call the deepest human damage. It distorts one of God's most special gifts.

Oh, how far people stray from God's purpose in all good things! We pervert His provision of nourishment for us by gluttony. We overload our senses and seek satiation in drugs and alcohol and mindless television. We numb ourselves to reality through every compulsive process we indulge in.

God reserved the gift of sex for the marriage relationship because of its importance to our most intimate self-concepts. Sexuality is the most vulnerable, the most private part of a person. And sex is the single most outstanding characteristic that sets apart the marriage relationship from other relationships. Which makes it all the more illuminating that human marriage is universally accepted as a picture of our relationship to God.

The church is called the bride of Christ. Bride—as opposed to helpmate or wife or matron or "old lady." A bride is a picture of purity and devotion and wholehearted love for the husband. She's also sexual. A virgin bride is brimming over with eager anticipation of fulfillment of her delayed sexual gratification. She awaits her honeymoon, a period of sexual activity rarely equaled in later years.

The Old Testament allows a full year for a honeymoon of withdrawal from social responsibilities and civic obligations. The new couple was encouraged to focus entirely on each other, to become intimately acquainted, to "biblically *know*" each other. Learning to give one another pleasure, to deepen the bond between them, was a responsibility that was especially blessed.

Translating that strength of intimacy into the comparable relationship with God shows how we are to desire Him and

236

delight in Him, as He desires and delights in us. So . . . is the intensity of sexual climax, the moment of deepest oneness between a couple, a metaphor for the transcendent fulfillment possible in our intimate communion with the Lord? Then God must be *pleased* with our orgasms, as an experience of a tiny insight into the surpassing exhilaration of truly knowing God!

How radically different a concept of sexual pleasure this is from the hopeless shame my inner child has always carried! Perhaps the writing I've done today is a step in the completion of God's work of healing my memories. Maybe He's going to simply give me new discernments to take in intellectually and incorporate gradually into my emotional understanding. I suppose that's enough. Not so dramatic as I imagined, but healing all the same.

Thank you, Lord.

Sunday, June 24, 3:30 A.M.

I was startled awake at 1:15 by the dog barking for no apparent reason. But there *was* a reason, because it was time for me to wake up, even though I'd only been asleep since 11:30. There was something more important to do.

I fought wakefulness for a little while, but I was getting part of a Bible verse in my head: "Jesus, the author, the finisher, the perfecter of our faith." I sleepily resisted what seemed to be simply a stray thought, until suddenly the word *finisher* resounded with added strength.

"Are we going to finish something now?" I thought. I decided to get up and write. I was excited about the possibility of the drama I'd been anticipating, and sleep was hopeless anyway.

I made myself a cup of tea, settled on the couch, and looked up the verse. It turns out I was hearing two translations mixed up together. "Looking unto Jesus the author and finisher of our faith" (Heb. 12:2 NKJV) and "Let us fix our eyes on Jesus, the author and perfecter of our faith" (NIV).

Funny, I never used to see any action from the Holy Spirit. Or hear God's voice. I didn't have enough faith. But Jesus is the author of the faith I have to see and hear Him now. And He's the one who woke me to finish this healing.

The habit I've developed this past year has been to write when I wake during the night. But instead, this time I switched off the lamp and just prayed. I saw that it was *judy* who needed to talk to God, not adult me.

So I asked her to climb the tree, and Jesus took off His sandals and joined her. There was a new addition in the branches, though. Jesus, the carpenter, had built a wooden platform so we could sit more comfortably than the tree limbs would allow. Maybe He expects us to use this platform for future conferences like this one, from time to time.

judy was still a little scared to be with Jesus all by herself. She began haltingly, but then her questions welled up and tumbled out of her mouth: *"Jesus . . . were you really there before I was born? . . . Did you really mean to make my body this way? Isn't it a mistake? It feels so bad and wrong! They made me so ashamed about having a vagina instead of a penis. I was ashamed of soft breasts and hips and that bloody mess every month. That was the worst! It must be a mistake!"*

Jesus didn't mind that she was crying. He held her and rocked her a little. "Yes, I was there. I had the pleasure of anticipating the woman you would become one day. I knit together your bones and sinews as you formed inside your mother's body."

She clung to Him and sobbed helplessly while He told her how He had watched her growing. "I directed the development of your ovaries and uterus—important parts of being female," He said gently. "I gave you a pelvis set wider than a male's, to shelter the developing babies you would someday be a mother to. Your reproductive system was designed for the miracle of birth, and it *was*, and *is*, very good."

"The blood is for a special cleansing, a preparation for the seeds of children to have a healthy place to take root and grow until the time is right for them to be born. It's all a part of the perfect plan for the female and male to complement each other in fulfillment of God's purpose for them to be fruitful.

"Have you forgotten, *judy*, that I was born of a woman? Mary's ovaries, like yours, produced eggs. One of those eggs was the seed of Christ. I was a baby carried in a uterus like the one I designed in you. I was delivered into the world through her vagina, in the midst of the nurturing blood that softened the walls of Mary's womb. Part of my purpose in entering the world through a natural birth was to show you the perfection of God's purpose in femaleness. There is no uncleanness in the blood."

I was surprised to recognize that Jesus was weeping with her. But then I could feel the surge of anger in His body, in the sudden clenching of the muscles in His shoulders and arms around her. He burst out, "How I *hate* the way they have hurt my children!" Then He took a deep breath and finally resumed His soothing undertone again.

"Your acceptance of your body's beauty has been corrupted by the shame of the evil that victimized you. The shame is a part of the curse sin brought into the world. I have no part of that! It belongs to their sin, not to you. Your body is the result of a perfect design."

She huddled in His arms, crying unashamedly for what seemed like a long time. Finally she found words to ask Him, "But . . . *what about pleasure?*"

He moved one hand to cradle her head as it rested against His chest. His fingers stroked her hair in that gesture of loving consolation she'd always wanted from Mama. I could see her hair shining in the moonlight. There were no tangles in it now, as it hung softly, long around her shoulders.

But now He was speaking in answer to her question. "When I made Adam, I knew it wasn't good for Him to be alone," Jesus said softly. "So I made Eve to be with him. Male and female were made for one another. Sexual pleasure was one of the ways for them to enjoy each other, to show love for each other. I gave them those wonderful feelings because I loved them so much. And I wanted them to know, from the strength of those sensations, that they had a Father who loved them enough to give such a special gift.

"I knew even then that sin would come into the world and cause strife between my children. I knew that husbands and wives would be driven apart, out of the pain sin brought. I wanted to help them stay together, for their own happiness. And divorces hurt Me, too, because I feel their anguish.

"Another reason I gave them pleasure, then, was to heal the wounds between them, to draw them together again and again in the oneness I intended them to enjoy . . . so they wouldn't hurt so much from the sin that kept pulling them away from each other. I never wanted them to feel so alone.

"I know what that aloneness feels like, you see. I lived a life of loneliness in my years on earth. I grieve for so many of my children who have been forsaken by others, as you have been, *judy*. So I intended the sexual relationship and orgasm to bond a husband and wife together as they would be bonded with none other. And in giving themselves intimately to one another, they could be drawn closer to Me and be comforted.

"The perfect nature of my design was not changed when human beings misused and perverted its purpose by victimizing you, *judy*. It is still a very good gift I have given you, in spite of the confusion that resulted from that evil. I will continue to remind you of its goodness, if you forget. Meanwhile, your mind and your heart are healing. And I am restoring your belief in your own purity."

They sat quietly in the tree for a few minutes while *judy* tried to take in the enormity of this love that accepted her so completely. She had never before experienced such complete acceptance or love. Which brought her to another question.

"What about Mama?"

Jesus' arms drew her closer to his heart. "Is she important?" he asked.

Suddenly, Mama didn't matter. *"No ... Mama never understood. Maybe she never will."*

"I long for your mother's healing, *judy*," Jesus said softly. He sighed. "But she has choices to make, just as you did. It will be up to her if it happens. You don't have to worry about that now."

"But I never had a mother who cared," she said sadly.

"You always had me," he answered. "You always will have me. I will be with you always, even to the end of the age."

Forever!

Jesus asked her if she could forgive Mama. It was easy to say yes. They talked about Jack and Gary and Richard and Hank and Carla. She was willing to let go of all of them, to forgive them.

God will heal any leftover feelings, but right now the past just doesn't seem very important. I guess the suffering was there for contrast, so I can see what the bright parts mean. It's all part of my life. So I don't regret the past.

Together, *judy* and I have a brand-new start. And there is such an incredible feeling of peace. I have an assurance of His presence and strength to accomplish what He wants my life to be. He's waiting in my tree any time I need help.

Thank you, God, for the love you've shown in my life. For the family you've given me in my husband and children. For

241

Jason, and the example he's been to me of Christ's compassion and acceptance. You've seen all my needs and provided for every one. You've given me painful catalysts and comforting relationships. And I can never be the same again.

Monday, June 25, 4:00 P.M.

As high as I was on Sunday morning with the elation of my healing, I have had such a feeling of weariness since then! I've been surprised by the sense of letdown and sadness. Despite a number of euphoric moments in prayer and in church, my general mood has been far lower than I would have anticipated. I guess I'm emotionally exhausted.

I've been disappointed in myself for not maintaining a positive attitude after such a powerful experience with God. I mean, how ungrateful can I get, to be depressed after Jesus personally took me in His arms and healed my wounds?

So I just dumped it on God this afternoon. I found myself saying, "God, I just feel so *weak!* I'm impatient and critical with the kids. I'm still withdrawn, when I have such different intentions. I feel as though what's ahead of me—healing my marriage and parenting relationships and the rest of your purpose for my life—is more than I can do, even after all the drama!"

And I was reminded of the song Jason sang with me: "Jesus loves me. . . . Little ones to him belong, they are weak but he is strong." Weak. *Weak* used to mean *bad.* But Paul said we can boast of our weaknesses because it is in our weakness that His strength is made perfect (2 Cor. 12:9). Haven't I admitted more than once that I'm powerless? I'm *supposed* to feel weak! Because that's what I am.

Having seen the magnitude of God's power in my life, can I have any hesitation in believing He will also provide a way for me to follow His will for the work still ahead of me? He is able to transform my weakness into His strength.

I'm still going to have times of withdrawing. I'll have moments and hours of depression sometimes. Behavior modification won't happen as fast as the spiritual surgery I'm recovering from. But I can trust Him to change me if only I do my part. I can give myself permission to be imperfect ... and weak. After all, weak people are the only ones He has to use.

Tuesday, June 26, 10:30 P.M.

Won't David be grateful when my sleep patterns eventually conform to "normal" expectations! Except for the occasional visit from the Lord, I don't wake up in the wee hours too frequently anymore, but I still have difficulty settling down at bedtime pretty often. So when I can't sleep, I still write instead.

We took a walk this evening after dinner and talked about my healing. David had read the journaling I did after the aftershock I experienced Saturday night/Sunday morning. He was pretty impressed. His attention had been drawn to the image Jesus gave me of menstrual blood—that it provides a special cleansing to prepare for conception.

"That really fits the consistent biblical image of blood as God's cleansing agent, doesn't it?" he said. Blood sacrifices in the Old Testament were representative of the covering over of sins so that God no longer saw them. But under the new covenant, Christ's blood purifies, washes away our sins, so they no longer exist at all between us and God."

I answered with a sudden new thought, "But what about the Old Testament references to a 'woman's time of uncleanness'?" I always resented those Scriptures! They reflected my own gut feelings about the shameful dirtiness of menstruation.

"Uncleanness is always the state before a time of purification, isn't it? Otherwise, what's the use of cleansing?"

243

Hmmm. So I am set to thinking. I guess if it's a process, it has a before and an after. If there's no uncleanness, there's no need for cleansing. Uncleanness is the state all of us are in except for Christ's blood, which cleanses us. But didn't Jesus tell me that there is no uncleanness in the blood? Oh . . . there is no uncleanness *in the blood!*

The blood itself isn't unclean. Does that mean female reproductive organs *are* unclean? That doesn't fit my new understanding of God's design for womanhood. This is beginning to look more complex, instead of simpler. *Help me, God. I'm confused.*

Only in the *Old* Testament, not in the New, were references made to menstruation as a time of uncleanness. Women had a special monthly cleansing, while at the same time, *all* the Jews were required to make regular, repeated blood sacrifices to cover their sins. After Christ's blood was shed to purify *all* uncleanness, once and for all, New Testament writers never referred to a woman as unclean, did they? No. Jesus' sacrifice purifies me as thoroughly as any male Christian.

But the monthly blood cleansing in women wasn't miraculously removed with Christ's sacrifice. Why? It must be a different kind of cleansing. It's not about spiritual cleansing to heal a spiritual imperfection which would make us unacceptable to God. It's only physical cleansing.

Well, now that I think about it, even the holiest of Christians still undergoes physical cleansing with soap and water. We don't connect sweaty bodies with moral pollution, do we? That would be absurd. Daily showers have to do with making human relationships more pleasant, not about being acceptable before God.

Then what about menstrual flow as cleansing? It doesn't have to do with social tolerance or spiritual acceptability. Is it a special kind of physical cleansing? Why?

Despite the fact that Christians are sanctified before God, we still live with the natural consequences of sin in the world. Because of sin, we have germs and disease and aging and death. We have social unrest and crime and suffering. And, more specific to this exploration, women have pain in childbirth and sexual dysfunction and menstrual cramps and PMS and "female problems." We have physical bodies that, though perfect in God's sight, are imperfect in their functioning.

God anticipated our physical imperfection after the fall, yet knew that a special environment, closer to perfection, was required for the beginning of new life. If babies could typically be conceived and develop to term in less than ideal uterine conditions, what chances for "normalcy" would those children have? Each set of parents would produce children whose own inherent human dysfunction intensified the physical anomaly in which they were formed. Like the inbreeding of royal families (incest again!) is said to have produced hemophilia, mental retardation, and insanity. If that was played out globally, the human race would decline to slobbering animalistic mutants within a few generations.

Instead, with statistically few exceptions, each human embryo is given a fresh start in a womb specially prepared for its presence, with more than "normal" physical soundness. If there is a malfunction in the menstrual cycle—a hormonal imbalance in the woman which would prevent the healthy development of a child—she generally experiences infertility. Wow! God set it all up so that, in spite of the effect of sin in the world, babies would continue to be born with ten fingers and ten toes, with their potential mental faculties intact. What a miracle!

God is present for each human beginning. And women are vessels of a holy event in conceiving a child. We are blessed to play a special role in the divine creation of a new life.

I could use the more standard word of *procreation* to label the occurrence of conception. But we get in the habit of seeing making babies as just a self-perpetuating process. It's all soiled by its association with our nasty, worldly concepts of sexuality. The only stain on the sexual union and creation of a baby is the one in our own corrupted minds. We've believed the lies Satan has fed us that sex is nothing more than a dirty joke.

Speaking of miracles, the radical change in my own understanding and acceptance of my physical form is nothing less than miraculous. I stand amazed at the gift of this insight that grew on the page in front of me. And I am humbled to be so blessed—to be a woman!

Friday, June 29, 8:30 P.M.

I shared my journaling about the healing with Jason in my session with him yesterday. He was pleased for me and thankful, that so much good has happened.

Tonight I was just thinking how very much of the writing I have done we haven't had time to discuss in the hours of therapy time. Jason has read most of my journals, but much of what I see as important growth hasn't ever been confirmed by Jason's expressed approval.

We couldn't cover everything I wrote this week, and I expect we probably won't manage to fit it in, ever. New issues are more important. But I just recognized the benefit of *not* talking it all through. I don't need Jason's initials on my insights. He doesn't have to confirm what I know to be my own growth, whether it comes from my own efforts or God's action. I can believe my own perceptions, whether Jason is ever aware of them or not.

The light dawns. Maybe this is what's known as self-esteem! If codependency is defined by its focus on other-, rather than self-awareness, then health must mean being my own interpreter and self-affirmer, rather than waiting for a grade from somebody else.

I guess it's about time. Having worked so hard, I think I can appreciate my own worth for putting forth the effort. I can look behind me and appreciate the journey itself. The experience of travel is just as important as the destination. Of course, the destination is only temporary, anyway. There will be more growth ahead of me my whole life. But I like myself the way I am today. It feels wonderful.

Sunday, July 8, 10:15 P.M.

Drum roll, please. Mom called me this afternoon. My last call to her was over seven months ago, and this is the first time she's called me. I was silent as she talked for a long time, just praying for words to use. I knew I didn't want to confront her yet, if ever. I *do* forgive her, but I still can't be with her, even by phone, and feel safe.

So when she finally faltered to a stop in recognition that I wasn't in the conversation, I began, speaking softly, slowly. "Mom, you know I've been seeing a therapist. I've had a very tough year."

"Yes?" I could hear fear in her voice.

"Well . . . I've been working on some very painful issues from my childhood. I'm at the point where I'm working on forgiveness, but I still need space to finish my healing. You've noticed that I haven't been in contact for quite a while. That's because being with family, even by phone, is still very hard for me. So I'm asking you to honor my need for detachment until I let you know I'm ready for communication."

There! I'd drawn a boundary, without abusing *her*.

There was a short silence, and then she asked carefully, "Was it something I did?"

I reminded myself to take a breath. "Mother, you did the best you could. Some things are handed down for genera-

247

tions, and we just don't know how to be any different than we are."

I can't remember anything more of the conversation. She didn't react with obvious anger or hurt. She was numb. Underneath, I know she was afraid. And by the time I hung up, I was shaking.

Now afterwards, I've been looking for anger that might have been resurrected by talking to her, after so long. I can't find any. What I see is my mother's wistful longing to give and receive love. She hurts so much that she can't feel anything else but her own pain. That's the story of her life.

The love she actually transmitted to her children was so small. But I can accept what was offered and forgive the rest. Forgiving Mom was the hardest of all, I think. Maybe that's why it's happening in stages.

I can love her, from a distance, keeping myself safe. I don't know when, if ever, I'll be able to spend time with her, but surely if God wants us to love our enemies, He'll give me grace to love my mother. She did what she knew how to do.

I had a talk about Mom with *judy*. She was sad. Still so sad. I told her, "Mama wasn't perfect, and she hurt us a lot, but it wasn't what she meant to do. Mama couldn't love us very much, and you needed to be loved, but God made up the difference . . . with grace. Amazing grace. You weren't an unloved child, *judy*. Some of us just need more grace than others. But you were never alone."

Mom's phone call was an opportunity to take stock of where I am. There's still a lot of sadness. Grief. But I can't find anger or shame or resentment. I don't think it's denial. It's healing. God has brought me to this point, light-years from the bitterness that used to consume me, so that I can experience freedom.

CHAPTER 15

Full Circle

My journey began with *judy's* old cringing: "I am bad—it's all my fault." My controlling outward focus on others was rooted in my defensive drive to camouflage my sense of "badness." In counseling I acknowledged my angry fixation on my own wounds: "They made me be who I am! How dare they hurt me so!" At last I arrived at adult accountability, learning to say quietly, "I am responsible for the pain of others, and I must expend my energies outward toward them, to do what I can to heal the consequences of my actions." Full circle, but my heart had changed. My caring for others could now spring from compassion, rather than compulsion to avoid my own pain.

Thursday, July 26, 9:30 A.M.

I dreamed this morning of being compelled to return to that old way of life. In the dream, I am forced at gunpoint into a panel van filled with abductees, all contentious strangers. Instantly I withdrew miserably inside myself, feeling isolated, different from the rest. They all seem to have memorized the weaknesses in their companions, and fire bitter epithets, aimed to strike at the most tender of wounds in one another. Why are they so infuriated at fellow victims? And they altogether ignore the captors, who smugly observe the hostility!

For tortuous hours, the van winds its way over rough mountain roads, until our arrival deep in the wilderness at what seems to be a secret field headquarters for a guerilla army. Sentries wearing plaid lumberjack shirts, blue jeans, and hiking boots greet each of the prisoners with suspicious glares and terse orders to stay with the group or face the consequences. The superficial peace and quiet of the heavily forested surroundings belie the hatred and fear that is almost palpable in the atmosphere.

Two sentries lead the group of prisoners, now mercifully quiet as they stare curiously at cabins and tents as we pass. Perhaps thirty men and women busy themselves around the compound; a group of burly men unload wooden boxes stenciled with arms-manufacturers' imprints—guns and ammunition—from a jeep pulled up at the back entrance of what appears to be a chapel.

I steal furtive glances at our captors, all dressed in similar outdoorsman-style clothing, but with a military bearing that sounds a warning not to question their dominance here. Clearly this is an army—in disguise perhaps—for a covert operation. I am chilled to recognize the deadly nature of their mission, from which they will not be long distracted.

My fellow-prisoners follow along, more like tourists after a guide than the hostages they are. Are they stupid? As we arrive at a dormitory-style cabin equipped with rough pine double-decker bunks, I fight back my own paralyzing fear to marvel at their apparent indifference to their captivity.

Discovering a color TV in one corner of the otherwise primitive communal room, they all rush to assemble on the benches arranged around the set. After some initial scuffling and cursing over the choice of programs, they focus on the screen, their faces immediately slack-jawed, dazed, as if drugged.

I climb, trembling, to an upper bunk, where I curl into fetal position to face the window view of a group of sentries who stand under a tree in grim conversation over clipboards and maps. Unexpectedly, one turns to cast a piercing glance up toward our cabin and directly into my eyes before I can react—too late—by squeezing them tight shut in feigned sleep. *I have been singled out!*

The group in front of the television squeals at some action on the screen, and I wonder at their apathy. Hadn't they been forced aboard the van, too? Hadn't they seen the barbed wire strung between the trees or the guns at the chapel? Whether they are pretending normalcy or are truly blinded to our endangerment, their behavior only serves to increase my sense of suppressed hysteria. Am I overreacting?

Suddenly I am aware of my daughter's presence beside me on the upper bunk. A wave of despair that she, too, has been captured threatens to undo the last vestiges of my composure. She is alarmed at my emotional state and tries to "jolly" me out of my bad mood. She accepts the performances of the others in the cabin and, like them, ignores the danger as if it doesn't exist.

I grip her arms, trying to convey to her that she must keep her head down, must not provide our captors with any reason to attack her. It is far too critical a time for hilarity ... our lives are at stake. As she resists my struggle to quiet her, she falls backwards off the bed.

She hits the floor with a loud thud, and I hear the snap of bone. Knowing I am responsible for her fall, I try to move to help her, but find myself paralyzed on the bed, strangling on the fear rising in my throat.

As she screams, the television-watchers crowd anxiously around her. "Oh, it's not that bad," they chorus. "Don't be so dramatic. Come watch TV with us—it'll take your mind off things. There's a good show coming on." Her screams quiet to helpless whimpers as they lead her away.

I awake in a cold sweat.

I shudder to reread what I have recorded here. How easy it was to question my own sanity in the midst of the denial of fellow captives of dysfunction. Until we can learn to face the painful truth, we cope by drugging our fear—numbing out with compulsive behavior. But we are all prisoners in the same concentration camp of generational evil. Even the church has been perverted to house weapons for the repression of prisoners, rather than sheltering the lost lambs Jesus came to save.

But most of all, I am struck with acute grief for my very real responsibility in hurting my children. One daughter in the dream represents both. Without intending it, I have passed on the chain of family pain to both of my daughters— in ways I can't see yet, and they don't feel safe enough to express. They have been abandoned by the effect of my emotional withdrawal and wounded by my chronic anger. I have been paralyzed by old fears which have overridden my puny impulses to comfort them.

Facing the fact that I am accountable for the damage in the lives of innocent children is so hard. Helping the process of healing their wounds will require me to become the kind of mother I always wanted for myself. I must give when I still want to receive, spend time with them when I want to withdraw. I must be patient with their needs when I want to lick my own wounds.

Part of me rebels at the work ahead of me still: *But I don't want to give them my time! Breaking old habits is too hard. I'm the one who's been working so hard for so long. Why does it still have to be me? I didn't get a childhood! Why should I work so hard for their childhood?"*

That's my inner child talking. She's jealous that they've already had a life so much easier than she ever had, and yet there are still changes to be made because I'm *not good enough* yet. She resents their needs when her own needs haven't been met.

Jason asked me if I had been jealous of my daughters. Blindly, I said no. But *judy* coveted every morsel of love they ever received. Is my inner child in competition with my daughters? Can't she learn to be friends with them? Even that is work.

So my basic selfishness comes into view. All my life I have focused on others for the purpose of distracting my own awareness of the pain inside me. It was always in the unacknowledged hope that others would love me and return the attention. So it was selfish. But now when I begin to see the real needs of my children and my real responsibility to meet them, I rebel.

I'm so tired! Can't I just think about me for a while? I don't want to be the strong one all the time. Just let me be a child. I never had the chance!

It's a tough assignment, and I'm not going to solve it in the next five minutes. But I will deal with it. Despite the whining of my inner child, I have come to expect integrity of myself. I won't shame her for her whining, but I won't run away from the challenge to face my responsibility.

Tuesday, July 31, 9:30 P.M.

Why do I keep thinking I'm finished with the tough assignments? How many more will there be?

Jason lit another fuse this afternoon when, in a conversation about healing the family, he asked, "What kind of father did your inner child expect David to be with your daughters?"

The detonation was instantaneous, and another brick wall came down, exposing a painfully defended truth. My inner child lived in the same house, slept in the same bed with someone she considered to be a convicted rapist . . . because in her mind, *all* men were convicted rapists. Had she known any other kind?

Over the years, watching the bond develop between David and our daughters was a constant reminder of her gut knowledge that men expect sex from little girls. Was David playing the "good father" only to lure them into an incestuous relationship? No! As I look carefully at the interactions I've seen between them, I can't believe he has ever been inappropriate with either of them. But my inner child is still afraid.

What did you think would happen, *judy*?

Daddies fool little girls into thinking they care. They make little girls need them, then they use their bodies for sex. That's what daddies do, and that's what little girls are for.

Oh, God, did I set them up? Did *judy's* expectation that incest was inevitable because little girls *are* victims enable

254

what might have happened, because she couldn't stop it? I *do not* believe it happened. But I can't take credit that it didn't.

Over the years, my chronic rage has shown up more in my relationship with my daughters than with anyone else. I've always had a hair-trigger temper, and my girls have received the brunt of my anger because *judy* felt safe to vent it on someone smaller. She couldn't be angry with David because he was a man and more powerful than she was. She expected him to hurt her . . . it wasn't safe to be mad at him. So she yelled at defenseless children.

The most difficult times to hold that anger in check have been at night. After dinner, my nerves were always strained to the breaking point by a full day of trying to control two little girls who wanted to be themselves, rather than the reflections of my will I demanded them to be. Every childish assertion of their independence threatened my tenuous grip on the control that held my sense of failure . . . of *badness* . . . at bay. By bathtime, my rage would be ready to erupt, unchecked. Shocked and angered, David soon took over evening parenting, and I would leave the room to cool off.

It became an assumed routine that David would be responsible for baths and tucking the girls into bed most of the time. Ashamed but relieved, I would withdraw to finish cleaning the kitchen and then to go for a walk. I always told myself it was because I had just run out of energy to deal with them. I was tired and stressed after a long day, and it gave David some quality time with them anyway.

But now I see with horror that I abdicated my role as mother-protector at exactly the time of day *judy expected* David to sexually abuse them. Her turmoil was the reason I would explode.

Bedtime is when it happens! It's going to happen and I can't stop it . . . just like I could never stop it happening to me. So don't make me be there to see it happen. Just let me be somewhere else.

Oh, *judy*! I abandoned my babies to David's care because my anxiety was too intense to keep inside. I purposely left my children with a man *judy* believed to be a convicted rapist, knowing unconsciously what he might do to them.

I let my daughters be human sacrifices to spare my own suffering. Anything to still *judy's* anxious voice in my head. Anything to keep the lid on my pain. I made the swiftest exit I could, over and over and over.

Just don't make me know it's happening.

I've done exactly what my mother did. She didn't let herself know it was happening, either, because she was hopeless to stop it. She kept herself safe at my expense.

I played the same role, and if my children haven't been abused, it's only because my husband didn't have the same script.

Every incest victim asks herself at some point, *Do mothers know?* I must answer, *mothers don't know until they finally <u>know</u>. And then maybe they discover that they knew all along.*

God forgive me.

Wednesday, August 1, 11:00 P.M.

I put in a call to Jason this morning. I thought I was past the panicky phone calls for reassurance. But the question kept pounding in my head: "Am I wrong in assuming David hasn't sexually abused them? Is there something there I can't see because of my own defenses?" I couldn't stand not knowing.

When Jason returned the call, despite my initial rush of words, I had trouble framing *the* question. "I've been processing what we talked about yesterday—that I expected David to abuse the girls—and you were right. *judy* assumed it would happen, and that's where a lot of my anxiety about parenting has come from, and why I've been so angry around bedtimes ..."

256

Finally I pushed past my fear to blurt out, "Could he have done that, Jason? Am I still in denial to think he didn't? Did I enable incest in my own family?"

"Judy, I haven't seen any evidence to lead me to conclude that David is a sexual abuser. The times I've met your girls I've observed their responses to me—a man—and I haven't seen any red flags. I can't give you guarantees at this point, but I think David would have already bailed out of his relationship with you if that's who he was."

I was limp with relief, but still searching for absolute confirmation. "Could he have been as supportive of my therapy as he has been . . . if he was an abuser?"

Jason gave a short laugh. "The sexually abusive men I've known could never have hung in there through this tough year with you like David has. Your therapy, and the degree that you've shared your memories with him, would have triggered his own memories. Seeing your pain would have been intolerable for a man carrying the shame of abusing his own daughters. No, I think not."

"Thank God," I murmured. But there was still the issue of my responsibility. I was glad to be on the phone with Jason instead of speaking in person. I didn't have to look him in the eye. "But I still played the same role my mother played! I'm just as guilty whether it happened or not. I set them up!"

He answered softly, "Judy, one of the things I really like about you . . ."

(I mentally interrupted to rebel at his approval of me: *He likes me? How can he like a person who could sacrifice her children like I did? I shouldn't be liked, I should be stoned!*)

". . . is your courage in facing the toughest issues. This *is* a hard one. But after you've processed it, I think you can find a way to forgive yourself for it and go on from there. You have been freed from the past that triggered those responses to your children. You're freed to love your daughters *now*. You can have a lot of hope for the healing of your family."

He talked about hope. I used to wish for my life and my family to be different. But I do have real hope now, rooted in a foundation of experience that real change is possible, however tough the challenge.

Yes, I will forgive myself. It's time for me to put the past behind me, to face the challenge of healing my family. *judy* still resists, but I can parent her as I parent my children. I don't *feel* ready yet, but I know that I wouldn't have recognized the task if it were not time to work on it. I have the tools for change, I just have to turn them to work outside myself, rather than inside. Lord, give me strength.

Thursday, August 16, 9:30 P.M.

My days are filled with a strange mixture of emotions lately. While I feel God's presence all around me, and am apt to cry tears of joy for His amazing goodness in my life, I alternately descend into profound loneliness. I still hunger for what I have lost.

As I look back at the former intensity of therapy, its progression seems independent of any agenda directed by Jason or myself. God must have been in charge. He daily gave me the lesson appropriate for that day, accompanied by the strength to deal with it. The assignments followed in the order I could accept and integrate them.

It has been as if, from the dark underwater depths of my soul, my painful issues have risen to the surface by a natural force of buoyancy unconnected to my effort or will. I've had a whole community—ha!—a metropolitan *complex* of assorted bundles of old trauma, each one firmly wrapped in layers of numbness and denial, chained by iron control and padlocked with repression to its own bolt at the bottom of the ocean that is my unconscious.

Gradually, over the past twenty-five years, the chains and locks had become encrusted with the barnacles and rust of bitterness and resentment. While the ever-thickening sedimentation held the bolts rigid in the bedrock, the iron control under the layers was weakening, eaten away by the rust. Then, last year, the shifting tides and currents in my relationships finally broke apart a crumbling link of one of the chains, abruptly freeing a bundle from its anchorage to rise with gathering speed up to the air and light.

Meanwhile, adrift in a tiny raft on the surface of the choppy sea, I was oblivious to the underwater drama . . . until the shocking surge of that first shameful bundle as it erupted from unconsciousness into conscious awareness bringing with it a storm of grief. I took hold of the package and, in spite of my dread at what I might find, I determinedly peeled back layer upon layer of numbness, then plunged my hands into slime accumulated over years of submersion. Deeper I probed, feeling my way, blinded by the tears and rain. Finally my fingers closed around one small object in the center of the ooze. I drew it out and held it up to wash it clean in the downpour of my tears. As the sludge melted away, I recognized the razor-sharp edges of an old block of crystallized anguish I had disowned long ago.

Time after time, more bundles of tormenting experience bubbled up into view, overwhelming me with renewed squalls of grief, rage, and yet more grief. But it was only in unwrapping and examining the contents, of welcoming those pieces of myself back home, that each storm abated, and there was peace in greater and greater measure.

However agonizing it has been to examine the wounds, I see at last that they are all buried treasure, and I've received comfort in accepting the hurts and releasing the shame. I have learned to cherish all those aching fragments of myself in order to find in them my long-lost purity and integrity. They are the feeling parts of myself that make me whole and healthy. Along with the grief, they contain my capacity to love and be loved, my empathy for others, my contentment. These were the qualities I saw in the lives of others, but secretly never believed could be elements of myself . . . until now. It is worth the pain to find the peace. Welcome home.